THE STUDENTS' SAUSAGE, EGG AND BEANS COOKBOOK

Jane Bamforth

foulsham
London • New York • Toronto • Sydney

foulsham

The Publishing House, Bennetts Close
Cippenham, Berkshire, SL1 5AP, England

For Dave, with all my love

ISBN 0-572-02621-8

Printed in Great Britain by Cox & Wyman Ltd, Reading

CONTENTS

JUST STARTING OUT?

So you're dying to take the kitchen by storm with one of the delicious recipes in this book? Before you begin, put the kettle on, make yourself a cup of tea and take a bit of time to read through the next couple of chapters – life in the kitchen will be so much easier once you've mastered the basics!

Whether you've just left home for the first time or are halfway through your college course, there's one thing for sure – you won't have much money to spare for food. But that doesn't mean you have to exist on beans on toast for all your student days. There are lots of easy ways to make sure you get a varied and healthy diet; and remember, a balanced diet doesn't have to mean a boring diet.

The recipes in this book range from soups through main courses to desserts and all contain at least one of the three main ingredients: sausages, eggs and beans. For more information on these turn to the next chapter. But first let's get down to basics ...

What should you be eating?

Try to eat at least five portions of fruit and vegetables a day to get a good balance of vitamins and minerals and lots of fibre. That may sound like a lot, but frozen, canned and fresh products and fruit juices all count. Try to include a couple of portions of high-protein foods a day for body growth and repair – take your pick from meat or fish or, if you prefer the vegetarian option, go for dairy products, such as milk, yoghurt and cheese, or pulses (beans and lentils). To maintain your energy levels and give you that 'full up' feeling, eat plenty of carbohydrate-rich foods such as rice, pasta, bread and potatoes.

And finally, a word of warning about fat and sugar - they're hidden in lots of ready-made, convenience foods, from yoghurts to cereal bars and crisps. Fat and sugar provide calories in foods but not much else and you can get what you need for energy from other foods, so when you're cooking go steady on oil, butter and sugar, and you'll be on the right track for a healthy start.

The vegetarian option

Obviously this is not a book for vegans as it contains a lot of dairy produce, but if you are a vegetarian or 'semi-veg', there are plenty of vegetarian sausages on the market so you can still enjoy the recipes. The texture of vegetarian sausages does vary, however, as some are slightly dryer and looser in texture than traditional pork sausages, so you might need to try a few different types in order to find the ones you like best.

The essential ingredients

If you keep a good stock of these basics then you'll always be able to throw together a quick meal without too much planning.

In the storecupboard
★ Pasta – choose a selection, but go for quick-cooking varieties if you can – save on your fuel bills too!
★ Plain (all-purpose) flour.
★ Rice – brown and white.

★ Red lentils – they don't need any soaking and can be added to thicken soups, stews and sauces to make them go further.

★ Salt and pepper – freshly ground black pepper gives the best flavour so buy whole peppercorns.

★ Stock cubes – vegetable, fish, beef and chicken (although you can use chicken with pretty much anything).

★ Vegetable oil – sunflower oil is fine for cooking, but if you want something a bit special for salad dressings, use olive oil.

★ Honey – the clear type is best, and apart from spreading on toast you can use it in stir-fries and oriental-style dishes.

Cans

★ Beans – check out the pulse guide on page 25.

★ Tomatoes – don't buy chopped tomatoes. They're more expensive and chopping them yourself is easy: just open the can, push the lid in and pour the juice out, remove the lid and chop the tomatoes in the can with a sharp knife.

★ Tuna in brine – much better for you than tuna in oil because it contains less fat.

★ Sweetcorn (corn) – add to risottos, pizzas and casseroles or use in fillings for baked potatoes or sandwiches.

★ Fruit – great for quick-and-easy last-minute puddings. Choose fruit such as apricots and pineapple in natural juice, without any extra sugar.

Fridge and freezer

★ Butter – more expensive than margarine, but it tastes much nicer with some foods, such as jacket potatoes, mashed potatoes and toasted tea cakes.

★ Cheese – buy strong-flavoured or mature cheese; you won't need to use as much to get a cheesy flavour, so in the long run it works out cheaper and better for you (you'll eat less cheese so less fat).

★ Eggs – buy medium-sized eggs.

★ Margarine or low-fat spread – look for one that you can use for cooking as well as spreading (check the label).

★ Milk – buy semi-skimmed milk; it's lower in fat than full-fat milk but it contains all the same nutrients and tastes good. Cartons of milk can be frozen.

★ Sausages (meat or vegetarian) – if you are lucky enough to have a freezer, buy the ones you can cook straight from frozen or loose-packed frozen sausages so you can just take a few out in the morning and leave them defrosting ready to cook later on.

★ Minced (ground) beef or Quorn – Quorn is a vegetarian alternative to mince made from myco protein from mushrooms; it is low in fat, high in protein and a good source of fibre.

★ Peas – frozen peas will fit into the smallest ice compartment so keep a pack handy for adding straight to soups or pasta sauces or using as an accompanying vegetable.

★ Bread and rolls – part-baked baguettes and rolls can be baked straight from frozen and remember you can toast frozen sliced bread if you forget to take it out of the freezer.

Fruit and vegetables
Try to keep a good selection of everyday fruit and vegetables – as well as adding variety to your cooking, they make good snacks and are certainly better for you than endless chocolate digestives!

★ Apples

★ Bananas

★ Green vegetables

★ Salad

★ Potatoes – when buying, choose potatoes with unblemished skins and pick out large ones for baking, rather than buying those packaged specially, as they're more expensive.

★ Carrots

★ Onions – if the recipe calls for half an onion, cut it in half before you peel it and wrap the other half tightly in clingfilm (plastic wrap); it will keep in the fridge for several days. If you are cooking for one, buy shallots and use just one or two instead of half an onion.

★ Cabbage – good shredded in salads as well as cooked.

Remember that salad and green vegetables should be bought fresh every few days but potatoes, carrots, onions, garlic and apples will keep for ages in a dry, dark place.

Herbs and spices

A sprinkling of dried herbs can really jazz up a plain dish, but you don't need to rush out and buy dozens of expensive little jars straight away. The ones listed below will be fine to get you started and then you can perhaps buy one a week, as and when you need them, to build up your collection.

Note that dried herbs can only be used in cooked dishes – if you want to garnish a dish with herbs, such as parsley, coriander (cilantro) or basil leaves, you must use fresh. These are fairly expensive to buy, but you can grow them very easily in a pot on your windowsill.

Dried herbs are much more pungent than fresh. 5 ml/1 tsp dried is equivalent to 15 ml/1 tbsp fresh.

★ Basil – the classic Italian herb to add to any Mediterranean-style recipe.
★ Mixed herbs – great for pasta sauces, cheese dishes and tomato dishes.
★ Parsley – add to soups and sauces.
★ Sage – goes really well with sausages, especially pork ones, and in risottos.
★ Chilli powder – this makes a good substitute for fresh chillies. Use chilli powder sparingly at first, to see just how hot you like your food! Different makes vary considerably in strength.
★ Curry powder – a ready-made blend of spices, ideal for quick curry recipes.
★ Cinnamon – a mild spice, delicious in apple puddings and savoury rice dishes. Buy the ground variety, not sticks.
★ Ground ginger – a tangy, distinctive spice. Try it in fruity puddings or stir-fries.

Sauces and relishes

A spoonful of something tasty is a great boost to many dishes, so gradually build up a stock of your favourites.

★ Chilli sauce – a traditional spicy Chinese sauce, good for stir-frying and marinating meat.

★ Mayonnaise – mix with crispy bacon, tuna, hard-boiled (hard-cooked) eggs or cooked meat for tasty sandwich fillings, or with chilli sauce, pesto or mustard for a dip (store in the fridge once opened).

★ Mustard – ready-made mustard is a mixture of spicy mustard seeds, vinegar and seasonings. Use it sparingly in salad dressings, cheese dishes and in meaty sandwiches to lift the taste.

★ Pesto – an Italian sauce made from basil, Parmesan cheese, pine nuts, olive oil and garlic. Stir it into cooked pasta for a quick meal or add a spoonful to soups and pasta dishes for a delicious flavour.

★ Soy sauce – a traditional Oriental sauce which adds a salty flavour to stir-fries, risottos and sweet and sour dishes.

★ Sweetcorn (corn) relish – great on burgers and with baked potatoes.

★ Tabasco sauce – an American spicy sauce – just add a few drops to spice up savoury dishes.

★ Tomato ketchup (catsup) – a classic that no student household should be without!

★ Tomato purée (paste) – a concentrated tomato paste to give lots of tomato flavour to soups and pasta sauces. If you buy it in a tube, it will keep for ages in the fridge and it is easy to use just the right amount.

★ Wine vinegar – a mild vinegar used in salad dressings.

Off to the shops

So you've read the recipe, you know what you need and you can't put it off any longer, but before you head out just bear in mind the following, so that you don't waste money:

★ Eat before you go shopping – otherwise you'll end up buying much more than you need!

★ Make a list – you won't forget what you went for in the first place and will avoid making impulsive, expensive buys.

★ If you've got a market nearby, go there first and you'll find a lot of produce (especially fruit and vegetables) is cheaper than at the supermarket.

★ Try to do a big shop once a week and avoid buying extra bits and pieces from corner shops – they are usually a lot more expensive.

★ Buy supermarket own-brand labels if you can.

★ Look out for offers on products you buy regularly (but remember, you're not saving money if you buy three cans of pineapple for the price of two if you only use it once a year).

★ Buy loose fruit and vegetables rather than prepacked – they are cheaper and you can see exactly what you're getting and after all it's not that difficult to wash and chop a few veg!

★ Ready-prepared meals are bad news – they're usually expensive, the portions are quite small and you can often make tastier dishes at home. It's tempting to opt for take-aways but try to avoid eating them too regularly as they're expensive, and just treat yourself occasionally!

The well-equipped kitchen

Right, so the cupboards are stocked with food, but have you got enough equipment to actually cook and eat your meal? Check out what your landlord has provided in the kitchen and then beg or borrow any of the following that you haven't got (kind relatives are good sources and if you have to buy, try jumble sales and charity shops!)

★ Plates, bowls and cutlery for everyone in the flat.

★ Three different-sized saucepans, preferably with lids, but you can improvise with foil if necessary.

★ Flameproof casserole dish (Dutch oven) with a lid – you can heat this on the hob and put it in the oven, and it can be used as an extra pan too.

★ Medium-sized non-stick frying pan (skillet) about 20 cm/8 in in diameter. Remember to use only wooden or plastic utensils on this and the surface should stay intact.

★ Baking (cookie) tray

★ Roasting tin (pan)

★ Two wooden spoons
★ Potato masher
★ Potato peeler
★ Fish slice
★ Large spoon
★ Plastic spatula
★ Small sharp knife
★ Large sharp knife
★ Can opener
★ Cheese grater
★ Corkscrew
★ Bottle opener
★ Whisk
★ Metal colander – this can be used to drain pasta, vegetables and rice and also as a steamer.
★ Sieve (strainer) – handy for draining small amounts of vegetables or to sieve (strain) a lumpy sauce.
★ Mixing bowl
★ Weighing scales
★ Measuring jug
★ Two chopping boards – use a wooden one for vegetables and cooked products and a plastic one for raw meat and fish.
★ Kitchen scissors
★ Tea towels (dish cloths) and washing-up cloths
★ Oven gloves

Saving energy

We're talking gas and electricity bills here, not how to cook without moving from the sofa! If you haven't had much cooking experience, it's worth bearing in mind the following points before you put the oven on every night for one jacket potato:

★ It's cheaper to use the hob than the grill (broiler).
★ Plan meals that don't need the oven, grill and hob at the same time.
★ Try not to put the oven on just to cook one dish. Either make a couple of dishes at the same time, or cook some jacket potatoes or roasted vegetables as well (see page 18), or cook

at the same time as your flatmates. Better still, make one big dish and share it.

★ Put lids on pans when you're bringing things to the boil.

★ Only boil as much water as you need in the kettle (most will boil just one mugful).

★ Make sure you match the size of the pan to the size of the ring. The heat from a large ring is just wasted on small pans and it will take ages for a large pan to heat up on a small ring.

★ Invest in a steamer, or use a metal colander – you can cook pasta or potatoes in the bottom saucepan and steam vegetables over the top at the same time, all on one ring!

Food hygiene

It's just not worth taking risks where food hygiene is concerned – you could end up feeling very unwell if you do. You have been warned!

★ Tidy up as you go along – it's much more hygienic, and less work, if you keep the kitchen as clean and tidy as possible.

★ Organise a weekly blitz – wipe the surfaces with anti-bacterial cleaner, empty the bins, sweep and wash the floor and have a general clean and tidy-up.

★ Try not to let your washing-up pile up in the sink – easier said than done for most students!

★ Always wash up with hot water (if there's none in the tank, boil a kettleful and mix it with cold).

★ Wash tea towels (dish cloths) and kitchen cloths regularly – they can be a breeding ground for bacteria.

Storing your food

★ Check packets and cartons for storage instructions, and make sure you store all perishables in the fridge; lots of items need to be stored in the fridge once opened, such as tomato ketchup (catsup), mayonnaise, salsa and pesto.

★ Never store half-used cans in the fridge. Empty the contents into a plastic container, preferably with a lid.

★ Always check the sell-by and use-by dates of foods when you buy them. Don't eat any food past its use-by date.

★ Store raw and cooked fish and meat separately. It's best to keep raw products, loosely covered or in a plastic box, on the bottom shelf of the fridge so that no drips can contaminate other food.

★ Put any leftovers in a clean container and, as soon as they are cold, store in the fridge. Do not put them in the fridge while they are still warm – the temperature of the fridge will rise and increase the risk of bacteria spreading to other foods.

★ Keep leftovers for a maximum of three days – try to eat them sooner but failing that throw them out.

★ Check packaging to make sure 'fresh' food hasn't been previously frozen; if it has, you can't freeze it again and you must eat it by its use-by date.

★ If you're cooking something from frozen, check to see whether you need to defrost it before cooking.

TIP: Save and wash up margarine containers and yoghurt pots with lids – they're useful for storing leftover bits and pieces in the fridge.

If you haven't done much cooking, don't panic – this chapter gives you a guide to basic cooking methods.

Pasta

Pasta is one of the easiest foods to cook. Just bring a large pan of lightly salted water to the boil, add a few drops of oil (this stops the pasta sticking together) and cook the pasta for the time stated on the packet. Use as required, either as part of a recipe or with sauce.

Rice

Whether you choose brown or white rice is really a matter of personal taste. To cook either type, bring a large pan of lightly salted water to the boil, add the rice and simmer for the time stated on the packet, drain and serve. White rice has had the bran layers and germ removed and takes 10–15 minutes to cook (check the packet for timings). White rice tends to be stickier than brown rice – rinse with boiling water when you're draining it to remove the starch that makes it stick together. Brown rice has only had the outer inedible husk removed; it has a higher fibre, vitamin and mineral content than white and takes 25–30 minutes to cook.

Arborio rice (a traditional Italian risotto rice) is slightly more difficult to cook: the liquid should be added gradually and absorbed a little at a time. It produces a very creamy result – check out the cheat's Sausage and Pepper Risotto on page 100 if you want to give it a go.

Potatoes

There are lots of different ways to cook potatoes – here are just a few to get you started.

Baked: Jacket potatoes are simple to cook – just scrub them, prick with a fork and pop in an oven preheated to 200°C/400°F/gas mark 6 for 1 hour or until cooked right through. Serve as an accompaniment to a main course or cut open, add a blob of butter and top with one of the following fillings: grated cheese, baked beans, tuna mayonnaise, crispy bacon, Curried Egg Mayonnaise (see page 63), Spicy Bean Salad (see page 54) – the possibilities are endless!

Boiled: Peel and chop the potatoes. If they are new, just scrub, then chop. Bring a large pan of lightly salted water to the boil, carefully add the potatoes and boil for 15–20 minutes or until tender. Drain well before serving.

Mashed: Cook as for boiled potatoes but don't use new potatoes as they should be peeled. For really fluffy potatoes, cover the pan of drained potatoes with a clean tea towel (dish cloth) for five minutes before mashing – this helps to absorb the steam. Add a little butter and milk and mash with a potato masher or fork until smooth. Beat with a wooden spoon until fluffy, season to taste and add more milk and butter if liked.

TIP: Add one of the following to jazz up plain mashed potato: 30 ml/2 tbsp pesto, 15 ml/1 tbsp made mustard, 2 crushed garlic cloves or a handful of grated cheese.

Rosemary potatoes

These are so easy and really delicious too!

Heat 60 ml/4 tbsp vegetable oil for 10 minutes in a roasting

tin (pan) in an oven preheated to 200°C/400°F/gas mark 6. Scrub potatoes and cut them into thick fingers and add to the oil. Shake the tin to coat the potatoes in oil and sprinkle over 10 ml/ 2 tsp dried rosemary. Season with salt and freshly ground black pepper and bake for 50–60 minutes, stirring occasionally to prevent the potatoes from sticking.
TIP: For a change, sprinkle over 2 crushed garlic cloves or 1 chopped chilli with the rosemary.

Root vegetables

Root vegetables such as carrots, swede (rutabaga) and turnips are all cooked in the same way as boiled potatoes – peeled, chopped and cooked in lightly salted boiling water. Carrots take 10–15 minutes and swede and turnip 15–20 minutes. Swede and turnip are best mashed with lots of black pepper and butter.

Punchnep

This is a traditional Welsh mash that goes really well with stews.

Cook equal amounts of potatoes and turnips in separate pans, drain and combine in one pan. Mash together with lots of butter, freshly ground black pepper and a dollop of cream.

Green vegetables

Green vegetables, such as broccoli, courgettes (zucchini), beans and mangetout (snow peas) can be steamed or boiled. Remember, the less time you cook vegetables for, the more nutrients are retained, so lightly cooked green vegetables are better for you. To steam, place a metal colander over a pan of simmering water, add the washed, chopped vegetables and cover with a lid. Steam for 3–6 minutes or until cooked to your liking. To boil green vegetables, cook the washed, chopped vegetables in boiling water for 5–8 minutes or until they are cooked to your liking.

Mixed vegetable dishes

We're not talking school-dinner-type mixed soggy peas, diced carrots and other unidentifiable cubes of vegetables – these are tasty, easy and healthy dishes with lots of texture and colour.

Stir-fries

Oriental-style stir-fried vegetables are easy to cook, but the preparation can take a little time. Cut the vegetables into bite-sized strips or pieces before you start cooking and then just keep adding to the pan. It's important to put in the vegetables that have the longest cooking time first.

Heat 15 ml/1 tbsp vegetable oil in a large frying pan (skillet) and add any of the following prepared vegetables (this order gives the slowest cooking vegetables first): onions, carrots, leeks, broccoli, French (green) beans, (bell) peppers, garlic, chillies, mangetout (snow peas), beansprouts and mushrooms, stirring continuously until all the vegetables are cooked. For an authentic Oriental flavour, stir in any combination of the following just before serving: 15 ml/1 tbsp soy sauce, 15 ml/1 tbsp clear honey, 5 ml/1 tsp ground ginger.

Roasted vegetables

If you've got the oven on to cook your main dish, cook a few vegetables in the oven at the same time, rather than using the hob for boiling or steaming.

Heat 30 ml/2 tbsp vegetable oil in a roasting tin (pan) in a preheated oven at 200°C/400°F/gas mark 6 for 10 minutes. Add a combination of the following prepared veg, chopped into bite-sized pieces: leeks, (bell) peppers, courgettes (zucchini), garlic, chillis, red onions (milder and sweeter than ordinary onions), aubergines (eggplants) and cook for 40–50 minutes until tender, stirring occasionally.

Eggs

See the following chapter for basic methods of cooking eggs.

Cheese sauce

It may seem odd to include this is in a guide to basic cooking, but a helping of cheese sauce with some boiled pasta or cooked cauliflower or a couple of hard-boiled (hard-cooked) eggs will make a quick, simple and substantial meal.

You can cheat and use granules or a packet to make the cheese sauce, but it's actually quite easy to make your own.

To make 300 ml/½ pt/1¼ cups of cheese sauce, melt 25 g/ 1 oz/2 tbsp butter or margarine in a small saucepan. Stir in 25 g/1 oz/¼ cup plain (all-purpose) flour, reduce the heat and cook the mixture, stirring all the time, for 1 minute. Gradually add 300 ml/½ pt/1¼ cups milk, stirring all the time to prevent lumps forming, until thickened. If you do end up with a lumpy sauce, simply sieve (strain) the sauce into a clean pan and gently reheat. Stir in 50 g/2 oz/½ cup grated cheese and season to taste with salt and freshly ground black pepper.

Variations

For a plain white sauce omit the cheese. For alternatives, add 10 ml/2 tsp dried parsley, 10 ml/2 tsp made mustard or 15 ml/ 1 tbsp tomato purée (paste) to the white sauce.

THE THREE MAIN INGREDIENTS

FEED ME

Always popular with students, sausages, eggs and beans are the basis of dozens of quick, easy and nutritious meals. Read on for a bit of inside info on the big three ...

Sausages

There are so many different types of sausages it can be a bit overwhelming when you're trying to decide which bangers to buy. From simple pork chipolatas to the more exotic varieties like beef and red wine sausages, you can use any type of sausage in the recipes in this book. Some types will work better than others, so experiment and see which ones you prefer. It is generally worth avoiding the very cheap varieties, as they often contain so much water that by the time you've cooked them there's not much left! Look for sausages with a meat content of over 70 per cent and you shouldn't go far wrong.

Although supermarkets offer a wide range of sausages, it is worth going to your local butcher to see what they stock too. The sausages may be a bit more expensive, but they are often made on the premises and it's worth splashing out for something special. After all, you only need a couple of really good sausages with a pile of mash and onion gravy (see page 116) to make a delicious meal.

Continental sausages

As well as the varieties of British sausage, you can buy lots of ready-cooked continental sausages now – check out the deli counter at your supermarket for the whole range. Here are just a few used in this book:

★ Chorizo – a spicy Spanish smoked pork sausage, flavoured with paprika and garlic. It can be eaten hot or cold and is sold sliced or as small, individual sausages.

★ Salami – a salted sausage, sold in slices and ready to eat. It is usually made from a combination of pork and beef and is often flavoured with garlic or peppercorns. Look out for Danish, Italian, German and French varieties.

★ Frankfurters – skinned individual sausages, sold in brine (salted water) in cans and jars or vacuum-packed. They are made from a combination of pork, chicken and beef and can be eaten hot or cold.

★ Smoked pork sausage – a large skinless sausage, which can be sliced or cut into chunks and eaten hot or cold. Look out for the garlic-flavoured variety, and if you want a healthier option go for the low-fat variety.

Vegetarian choice

There's a wide selection of good vegetarian sausages available now. They're usually made from a combination of soya bean curd, soya beans and vegetable protein. They all differ slightly in taste and texture, so the best bet is to try a few different types until you find one you really like. And don't forget to check out frozen veggie sausages – they are often the best kind. All of the recipes in this book work just as well with veggie sausages as meat ones, but the cooking times will probably need to be reduced by a few minutes – keep checking them until they are cooked through.

TIP: The British Sausage Appreciation Society was set up in 1991 for sausage lovers everywhere! As a member, you can keep up to date with the latest sausage news and receive free goodies and information. If you would like to join the society (it's free!), send a stamped, addressed envelope to Alison Cook, BSAS, PO Box 44, Winterhill House, Snowdon Drive, Milton Keynes MK6 1AX.

Cooking sausages

There are three basic ways of cooking sausages: grilling (broiling), frying (sautéing) and baking. Obviously cooking times will vary slightly, depending on the type of sausage but always make sure they are cooked right through and piping hot before you eat them. Sausages bought frozen can be cooked straight from the freezer, but if you've bought sausages and frozen them yourself make sure they are thoroughly defrosted before cooking.

Grilling: Preheat the grill (broiler) to medium. Place the sausages on the grill pan and cook for 12–15 minutes, turning every few minutes.

Frying: Not as healthy as grilling, but if you fancy a fry-up occasionally, go for it! Heat 15 ml/1 tbsp oil in a frying pan (skillet). Cook the sausages gently in the oil for 12–15 minutes, turning frequently.

Baking: This is a good method to use if you're cooking something else in the oven but it's not worth putting the oven on just to cook a couple of sausages! Preheat the oven to 190°C/375°/gas mark 5, place the sausages on a baking (cookie) tray and cook for 30–40 minutes, turning halfway through the cooking time.

Eggs

Eggs are one of the most natural convenience foods available, providing us with proteins, fats, vitamins and minerals. Unfortunately, they also contain cholesterol, a by-product of animal fats that is often cited as contributing to heart disease, so you should try not to eat them every day.

Eggs should be kept in the fridge and can be used for most cooking when they are cold, but if you are going to whisk one, say for a chocolate mousse, take it out of the fridge in time to come to room temperature before you start.

There are lots of ways to cook eggs, but here are four of the most basic methods.

Fried (sautéed): Heat 15 ml/1 tbsp vegetable oil in a frying pan (skillet) over a medium heat. Break the egg into the frying pan and spoon the hot fat over – the egg will start to set straight away. Fry for 3–5 minutes or until the white is firm.

Scrambled: Allow 2 eggs per person, and beat well with salt and pepper. Melt 15ml/1 tbsp butter or margarine in a small pan. Pour the beaten eggs into the pan and cook slowly, stirring all the time until they begin to thicken. When the egg mixture is still slightly liquid, remove from the heat and continue to beat; the heat of the pan will finish the cooking process. Add extra butter or 15 ml/1 tbsp cream for an extra creamy texture.

Soft-boiled: Bring a small pan of cold water to the boil, then reduce to a gentle simmer. With a spoon, carefully lower the eggs into the pan. Simmer for 1 minute, then remove the pan from the heat. Put a lid on the saucepan and leave the eggs for 5–6 minutes. The yolk should be soft and creamy and the white just set.

Hard-boiled (hard-cooked): Place the eggs in a small saucepan of water, bring to the boil and simmer for 6–7 minutes, then remove from the heat and plunge the eggs into cold water immediately. This stops the eggs from continuing to cook and prevents a black ring forming round the yolks. To shell the eggs, tap gently to crack the shell, peel it away and then rinse under cold running water to remove any traces of shell before serving.

Omelettes

There are two types of omelette – rolled omelettes (see below), which are usually individual omelettes with a filling and open omelettes, or tortillas, which contain lots of filling ingredients incorporated into the egg.

Rolled omelette: Heat 15 ml/1 tbsp vegetable oil in a 15–20 cm/6–8 in frying pan (skillet). Beat 2 eggs and season. Pour the eggs into the pan and swirl them around until the base is covered with egg. Gently push the edges of the omelette in a little and swirl the pan again to cover the edges with egg.

Continue until the surface of the omelette is just set. Top with your chosen filling (see below).

★ Cooked bacon, chopped into pieces
★ 30 ml/2 tbsp grated cheese or cream cheese
★ Mushrooms, sliced and cooked in a little oil
★ Sliced (bell) pepper, fried (sautéed) in a little oil
★ 15 ml/1 tbsp pesto, spread over the omelette
★ Cooked, diced potato
★ Flaked, canned tuna mixed with mayonnaise

Fold the omelette in half and slide on to a plate. Serve with crusty bread and a salad for a quick and easy filling meal.

Poached eggs

Pour 3 cm/1¼ in water into a small saucepan and bring to a gentle simmer. Break an egg into a cup and pour it carefully into the water. Cook for 3 minutes, occasionally spooning water over the egg to help the cooking process. Remove with a slotted spoon and place on kitchen paper (paper towels) to remove any excess water before serving.

Beans

Beans are part of the pulse family, which includes many types of beans, peas and lentils that have been preserved by drying. Pulses are a major part of any vegetarian diet because they are a good source of protein. Many students avoid pulses with the possible exception of baked beans in tomato sauce and kidney beans in chilli. But they are cheap, easy to use and, as well as giving distinctive individual flavours to dishes, they are great for making stews, soups and sauces go just a little bit further.

The extra good news is you don't have to soak them overnight and then cook them for hours (that is unless you can be bothered!) because there is a wide selection of ready-to-eat canned beans, peas and lentils available. So steer clear of dried pulses with the exception of red lentils, which can be cooked without any soaking – it's a whole lot easier to open a can!

The great pulse guide

There are so many different types of pulses, it would be impossible to list them all, but here are the ones used in this book.

★ Borlotti beans – an oval-shaped, pale brown, plump bean that has a sweet flavour with a creamy, smooth texture. Great in salads, bakes and casseroles.

★ Butter (lima) beans – large, white beans that have a rich creamy, texture. Good in bean salads, with chicken dishes and in soups.

★ Cannellini beans – a type of haricot (navy) bean, they are slender, cream-coloured beans with a firm texture. Used in Italian-style soups, stews and pasta dishes.

★ Chick peas (garbanzos) – these pale golden peas have a rich nutty flavour and firm texture. Used in traditional Middle Eastern dishes such as hummus and falafels, also good in curries.

★ Flageolet beans – pale green beans with a subtle, nutty taste. Good for adding flavour and colour to vegetarian stews and soups.

★ Red kidney beans – these red, kidney-shaped beans have a firm texture and distinctive flavour. Used in dishes like Chilli con Carne (see page 85) and also good for adding colour to salads.

★ Red lentils – small, round, split lentils, great for thickening soups and sauces. These lentils reduce to a purée when cooked with water for 15–20 minutes.

NOTES ON THE RECIPES

FEED ME

★ Do not mix metric, imperial and American measures. Follow one set only.
★ All spoon measurements are level.
★ All eggs are medium.
★ Always wash, peel and core, where necessary, fruit and vegetables before use, unless otherwise stated.
★ Can and packet sizes are approximate – they will differ slightly from brand to brand.
★ All preparation and cooking times are approximate – everyone works at a different speed in the kitchen.
★ I have usually used dried herbs as these are less expensive and wasteful than fresh (the exception being herbs for garnishing where only fresh will do). If you wish to substitute fresh for dried, 5 ml/1 tsp dried = 15 ml/1 tbsp fresh. Do not substitute dried where fresh are called for.
★ I have given the number of servings for each recipe, but bear in mind that appetites vary!
★ You can alter the number of servings by doubling or halving ALL the quantities in a recipe. You can save on fuel bills (and

effort!) by cooking larger quantities and either freezing the extra portions or keeping them in the fridge to be eaten later in the week. Don't try to freeze cooked pasta, however, and don't keep leftovers for more than three days.

★ Read the recipe right through to check you have everything you need before starting to cook – then you can assemble the ingredients and equipment before you get your hands dirty.

★ Always preheat the oven and cook on the centre shelf (remember electric ovens usually take longer to heat up than gas ovens).

★ All ovens vary (especially those in student houses). If dishes always seem to be overdone, reduce the heat by 10°C/25°F/gas mark 1 or, if they seem to take longer than they should to cook, increase the heat by the same amount. And it's worth remembering that the top of the oven is likely to be hotter than the bottom.

★ You'll find a range of simple and tasty desserts in the chapter on entertaining which starts on page 131.

SOUPS

FEED ME

Forget canned or packet soups and have a go at making your own; you can't beat a bowl of home-made soup for a cheap meal. All the recipes in this chapter are for main-course soups – if you want to serve the soup for a lighter lunch or snack, just add more liquid at the end of the cooking time to get the consistency you want.

The soups in this chapter will keep for up to three days in the fridge. If you've still got some left over after that, simply pour into a freezerproof container and freeze for up to three months. To reheat, allow to defrost thoroughly, then heat gently in a pan until piping hot; add water if the soup seems too thick.

All you need to accompany your soup is a hunk of crusty bread (see page 39) or a roll. But for a special touch, try making your own croûtons: cut a couple of slices of bread into cubes and fry (sauté) in hot oil until golden. For garlic and herb croûtons, sprinkle the bread with 1 crushed garlic clove and 2.5 ml/½ tsp dried mixed herbs before cooking.

TOMATO AND BEAN SOUP

Serves 2

Ingredients	Metric	Imperial	American
Vegetable oil	15 ml	1 tbsp	1 tbsp
Onion, chopped	1	1	1
Garlic clove, crushed	1	1	1
Can of tomatoes, chopped	400 g	14 oz	1 large
Can of cannellini beans, drained	400 g	14 oz	1 large
Chilli powder (optional)	5 ml	1 tsp	1 tsp
Dried basil	5 ml	1 tsp	1 tsp
Sugar	5 ml	1 tsp	1 tsp
Water	300 ml	½ pt	1¼ cups
Salt and freshly ground black pepper			
Grated cheese and crusty bread, to serve			

1   Heat the oil gently in a medium pan, add the onion and garlic and fry (sauté) over a medium heat for 3–5 minutes until soft.

2   Add the remaining ingredients, cover and cook over a medium heat for 15–20 minutes, stirring occasionally.

3   Season to taste with salt and pepper, top with grated cheese and serve with crusty bread.

)》 Preparation time: 10 minutes
Cooking time: 20 minutes

TIP: If you don't have a garlic crusher, use the blade of a large knife to flatten the garlic and then chop it finely.

SPICY LENTIL BROTH

Serves 2

Ingredients	Metric	Imperial	American
Vegetable oil	30 ml	2 tbsp	2 tbsp
Onion, chopped	1	1	1
Can of tomatoes, chopped	400 g	14 oz	1 large
Red lentils	100 g	4 oz	⅔ cup
Chilli powder	10 ml	2 tsp	2 tsp
Water	600 ml	1 pt	2½ cups

Salt and freshly ground black pepper

1   Heat the oil in a medium pan, add the onion and fry (sauté) over a medium heat for 3–5 minutes until soft.

2   Add the tomatoes, lentils, chilli powder and water. Stir well, cover, bring to the boil, then simmer for 20–25 minutes. Season to taste with salt and pepper.

Preparation time: 2 minutes
Cooking time: 25 minutes

TIP: Serve this with a swirl of yoghurt or cream and a sprinkling (no more!) of chilli powder.

30

CHUNKY FISH SOUP

Coley is similar to cod but much cheaper. Any white fish (such as cod, haddock, hake or whiting) works well in this recipe – use whatever is cheapest.

Serves 2

Ingredients	Metric	Imperial	American
Vegetable oil	30 ml	2 tbsp	2 tbsp
Leek, sliced	1	1	1
Celery sticks, chopped	2	2	2
Potato, diced	1	1	1
Garlic cloves, crushed	2	2	2
Can of tomatoes, chopped	400 g	14 oz	1 large
Fish stock	600 ml	1 pt	2½ cups
Can of cannellini beans, drained	400 g	14 oz	1 large
Dried parsley	10 ml	2 tsp	2 tsp
Salt and freshly ground black pepper			
Coley, skinned and cubed	350 g	12 oz	12 oz

1 Heat the oil in a large pan and fry (sauté) the leek, celery, potato and garlic for 5 minutes, stirring continuously.

2 Add the tomatoes, stock, beans and parsley, and season to taste with salt and pepper. Bring to the boil, then simmer gently for 10 minutes.

3 Add the fish and cook for another 10 minutes or until the fish flakes easily.

Preparation time: 10 minutes
Cooking time: 20 minutes

CHICK PEA AND CORIANDER SOUP

Serves 2

Ingredients	Metric	Imperial	American
Vegetable oil	15 ml	1 tbsp	1 tbsp
Onion, chopped	1	1	1
Garlic cloves, crushed	2	2	2
Can of chick peas (garbanzos), drained	400 g	14 oz	1 large
Dried coriander (cilantro)	10 ml	2 tsp	2 tsp
Salt and freshly ground black pepper			
Vegetable stock	900 ml	1½ pts	3¾ cups

1 Heat the vegetable oil in a medium pan, add the onion and garlic and cook for 3–5 minutes until soft.

2 Mash the chick peas, using a fork or potato masher. Add to the pan, stirring well, then add the coriander and season with salt and pepper. Gradually add the stock, stirring all the time. Bring to the boil, then simmer for 15–20 minutes.

 Preparation time: 10 minutes
Cooking time: 20 minutes

MINESTRONE SOUP

Serves 4

Ingredients	Metric	Imperial	American
Vegetable oil	15 ml	1 tbsp	1 tbsp
Onion, chopped	1	1	1
Garlic clove, crushed	1	1	1
Celery sticks, chopped	2	2	2
Can of tomatoes, chopped	400 g	14 oz	1 large
Dried mixed herbs	10 ml	2 tsp	2 tsp
Green (bell) pepper, diced	½	½	½
Carrot, diced	1	1	1
Vegetable stock	900 ml	1½ pts	3¾ cups
Can of cannellini beans, drained	400 g	14 oz	1 large
Salt and freshly ground black pepper			
Spaghetti	25 g	1 oz	1 oz

1   Heat the oil in a large saucepan and fry (sauté) the onion, garlic and celery for 5 minutes until soft.

2   Add the tomatoes, mixed herbs, vegetables, stock, beans and seasoning, bring to the boil, then cover and simmer for 30 minutes.

3   Add the spaghetti, broken into short lengths, return to the boil, then simmer, uncovered, for 10 minutes. Check the seasoning before serving.

)) Preparation time: 10 minutes
   Cooking time: 40 minutes

WINTER VEGETABLE SOUP

Serves 2

Ingredients	Metric	Imperial	American
Vegetable oil	15 ml	1 tbsp	1 tbsp
Onion, chopped	1	1	1
Garlic clove, crushed	1	1	1
Carrot, sliced	1	1	1
Parsnip, sliced	1	1	1
Potato, diced	1	1	1
Leek, sliced	1	1	1
Stock	900 ml	1½ pts	3¾ cups
Can of butter (lima) beans, drained	400 g	14 oz	1 large
Dried thyme	5 ml	1 tsp	1 tsp
Grated cheese and wholemeal rolls, to serve			

1 Heat the oil in a large saucepan, fry (sauté) the onion and garlic for 3–5 minutes until soft.

2 Add the remaining ingredients, stir well and season with salt and pepper. Bring to the boil, then reduce the heat, cover the pan and cook for 30–35 minutes until the vegetables are tender.

3 Top with grated cheese and serve with warm wholemeal rolls.

)) Preparation time: 10 minutes
Cooking time: 35 minutes

BORLOTTI BEAN AND BACON SOUP

Serves 2

Ingredients	Metric	Imperial	American
Vegetable oil	15 ml	1 tbsp	1 tbsp
Onion, chopped	1	1	1
Bacon rashers (slices), rinded and chopped	6	6	6
Can of borlotti beans, drained	400 g	14 oz	1 large
Red lentils	15 ml	1 tbsp	1 tbsp
Stock	1.2 litres	2 pts	5 cups
Tomato purée (paste)	30 ml	2 tbsp	2 tbsp
Dried parsley	5 ml	1 tsp	1 tsp
Salt and freshly ground black pepper			

1 Heat the oil in a large saucepan and fry (sauté) the onion for 3 minutes until soft.

2 Add the chopped bacon and fry for 5 minutes, stirring occasionally.

3 Add the remaining ingredients, bring to the boil, then reduce the heat and cook for 20 minutes. Season to taste with salt and pepper before serving.

 **>» Preparation time: 10 minutes
Cooking time: 20 minutes**

HAM AND LENTIL SOUP

Serves 2

Ingredients	Metric	Imperial	American
Vegetable oil	15 ml	1 tbsp	1 tbsp
Onion, chopped	1	1	1
Garlic clove, crushed	1	1	1
Can of tomatoes, chopped	400 g	14 oz	1 large
Red lentils	50 g	2 oz	⅓ cup
Dried parsley	5 ml	1 tsp	1 tsp
Water	600 ml	1 pt	2½ cups
Ham, diced	75 g	3 oz	¾ cup

Salt and freshly ground black pepper

1 Heat the oil in a large saucepan, fry (sauté) the onion and garlic for 3–5 minutes until soft.

2 Add the tomatoes, lentils, parsley and water. Bring to the boil, stir well, then cover and simmer for 20 minutes.

3 Add the ham and cook for a further 5 minutes. Season to taste with salt and pepper before serving.

 Preparation time: 10 minutes
Cooking time: 25 minutes

CHILLI BEAN SOUP

Make this with minced (ground) beef and beef stock, or for a vegetarian version use Quorn and vegetable stock. For a special touch, serve with a dollop of plain yoghurt and a spoonful of salsa.

Serves 2

Ingredients	Metric	Imperial	American
Vegetable oil	15 ml	1 tbsp	1 tbsp
Onion, chopped	1	1	1
Garlic clove, crushed	1	1	1
Minced beef or Quorn	100 g	4 oz	4 oz
Red (bell) pepper, chopped	½	½	½
Green pepper, chopped	½	½	½
Can of tomatoes, chopped	400 g	14 oz	1 large
Beef or vegetable stock	600 ml	1 pt	2½ cups
Dried mixed herbs	5 ml	1 tsp	1 tsp
Chilli powder	5 ml	1 tsp	1 tsp
Can of kidney beans, drained	200 g	7 oz	1 small
Salt and freshly ground black pepper			

1 Heat the oil in a large saucepan and fry (sauté) the onion and garlic for 3–5 minutes until soft.

2 Add the minced beef or Quorn and cook for 5 minutes.

3 Add the remaining ingredients and season with salt and pepper. Bring back to the boil, cover and simmer for 30 minutes. Adjust the seasoning, if necessary, then serve.

)) Preparation time: 10 minutes
Cooking time: 30 minutes

CURRIED BAKED BEAN SOUP

Serves 2

Ingredients	Metric	Imperial	American
Vegetable oil	15 ml	1 tbsp	1 tbsp
Onion, chopped	1	1	1
Curry powder	10 ml	2 tsp	2 tsp
Tomato purée (paste)	15 ml	1 tbsp	1 tbsp
Can of baked beans in tomato sauce	400 g	14 oz	1 large
Vegetable stock	600 ml	1 pt	2½ cups
Salt and freshly ground black pepper			
Naan bread, to serve			

1 Heat the oil in a saucepan and fry (sauté) the onion for 3–5 minutes until soft.

2 Add the curry powder and tomato purée, stir well and cook for 1 minute.

3 Add the beans and stock, season to taste and bring to the boil. Reduce the heat and simmer for 10–15 minutes.

4 Serve with warmed naan bread.

Preparation time: 5 minutes
Cooking time: 15 minutes

TASTY ACCOMPANIMENTS

To make a bowl of soup into a filling main course, serve with lots of warm bread and some cheese. There are lots of different types of bread available, so don't just stick to sliced white, try one of the following:

★ **Ciabatta:** A flat Italian bread with a chewy texture and a crispy crust.

★ **Focaccia:** A soft, round Italian bread often flavoured with garlic or herbs.

★ **Sfilatino:** An Italian-style baguette made with olive oil, with a crispy crust and soft centre.

★ **Flavoured breads:** You can buy bread with cheese, pesto, sun-dried tomatoes, garlic and herbs, onion, olives ... the list is endless, so check out your local bakers and see what they've got on offer.

★ **Baguette:** Don't forget that old French favourite! Eat it plain, or jazz it up (see below).

★ **Cheese slices:** Slice a baguette and toast the slices, sprinkle with grated cheese and grill (broil) until golden brown. Serve on side plates or float the cheesy slices in the soup.

★ **Garlic bread:** Slice a baguette, taking care not to cut through the bottom crust. Spread between the slices with a paste made from 2 crushed garlic cloves and 50 g/2 oz/¼ cup of butter or margarine. Wrap in foil and heat in the oven for 10 minutes at 180°C/350°F/gas mark 4.

For those late mornings (or early afternoons) when a bowl of cereal isn't going to do the job, try one of these quick and easy ideas to keep you going until dinner.

SPANISH OMELETTE

This omelette is just as good served hot or cold.

Serves 2

Ingredients	Metric	Imperial	American
Vegetable oil	30 ml	2 tbsp	2 tbsp
Onion, chopped	1	1	1
Cooked potatoes, cubed	225 g	8 oz	8 oz
Green (bell) pepper, chopped	½	½	½
Eggs, well beaten	4	4	4
Salt and freshly ground black pepper			
Dried parsley	5 ml	1 tsp	1 tsp
Cheddar cheese, grated	100 g	4 oz	1 cup

1 Heat the oil in a 20–25 cm/8–10 in flameproof frying pan (skillet), add the onion and fry (sauté) over a medium heat for 3–5 minutes. Add the potatoes and pepper and cook for 5 minutes, stirring occasionally.

2 Season the eggs with salt and pepper and stir in the parsley. Pour over the vegetable mixture and cook for 2–3 minutes until the base is set.

3 Sprinkle over the cheese and grill (broil) under a preheated grill (broiler) for 3–4 minutes until golden brown. Serve cut into wedges.

Preparation time: 5 minutes
Cooking time: 12 minutes

BAKED EGGS

If you don't have any ramekins (custard cups), use ovenproof cups. Alternatively, bake the eggs in mugs, with the water coming only about halfway up the mugs.

Serves 1

Ingredients	Metric	Imperial	American
Butter or margarine	30 ml	2 tbsp	2 tbsp
Eggs	2	2	2
Salt and freshly ground black pepper			
Crispy bacon and hot buttered toast, to serve			

1 Place two small ovenproof ramekins on a baking (cookie) tray. Place half the butter or margarine in each dish and put in a preheated oven at 180°C/350°F/gas mark 4 for 2 minutes to melt.

2 Break an egg into each dish and season well with salt and pepper. Place the ramekins or cups in a roasting tin (pan), fill the tin with hot water to within 1 cm/½ in of the rims of the dishes, cover the tin with foil and bake for 8–10 minutes or until cooked to your liking.

3 Loosen the eggs with a knife, then turn out on to a plate and serve with crispy bacon and hot, buttered toast.

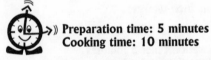 Preparation time: 5 minutes
Cooking time: 10 minutes

TIP: For a more filling meal, sprinkle a layer of grated cheese, cooked vegetables, meat or fish in the base of the dishes before you add the eggs.

CHORIZO TORTILLA

Chorizo is a spicy Spanish pork sausage, flavoured with paprika (a mild pepper). If you can't find it in your local shop, used cooked, sliced, herby pork sausages instead.

Serves 2

Ingredients	Metric	Imperial	American
Vegetable oil	30 ml	2 tbsp	2 tbsp
Chorizo, sliced	150 g	5 oz	5 oz
Onion, chopped	1	1	1
Eggs, beaten	4	4	4
Salt and freshly ground black pepper			
Cheddar cheese, grated	75 g	3 oz	¾ cup

1 Heat the vegetable oil in a 20–25 cm/8–10 in frying pan (skillet), add the chorizo and onion and fry (sauté) for 5 minutes until soft.

2 Season the eggs and pour over the sausage and onion mixture. Cook for 2–3 minutes until the base is set.

3 Sprinkle over the cheese and grill (broil) under a preheated grill (broiler) for 3–4 minutes or until golden brown.

Preparation time: 5 minutes
Cooking time: 7–8 minutes

BREAKFAST SCRAMBLE

Serves 2

Ingredients	Metric	Imperial	American
Butter or margarine	25 g	1 oz	2 tbsp
Green (bell) pepper, chopped	1	1	1
Eggs	4	4	4
Milk	75 ml	5 tbsp	5 tbsp
Salt and freshly ground black pepper			
Ham, chopped	50 g	2 oz	½ cup
Slices of bread, toasted	4	4	4
Cheddar cheese, grated	50 g	2 oz	½ cup

1 Melt the butter or margarine in a frying pan (skillet) and fry (sauté) the green pepper for a few minutes until soft.

2 Beat the eggs and milk together, add a little salt and pepper, then pour over the green pepper and stir slowly over a gentle heat until almost cooked. Stir in the ham and cook gently until set.

3 Top the toast with the scrambled egg, sprinkle with cheese and serve.

Preparation time: 5 minutes
Cooking time: 5–10 minutes

TIP: For a vegetarian version, omit the ham and stir in some cooked vegetables – potatoes, onions and leeks all work well.

NAAN SAUSAGE BRUNCH

Serves 1

Ingredients	Metric	Imperial	American
Large naan bread	1	1	1
Tomato ketchup (catsup)	15 ml	1 tbsp	1 tbsp
Made mustard	2.5 ml	½ tsp	½ tsp
Onion	½	½	½
OR Shallots	1–2	1–2	1–2
Mushrooms	2	2	2
Tomato	1	1	1
Salt and freshly ground black pepper			
Pork sausages	2	2	2
Bacon rashers (slices), rinded	1	1	1

1 Place the naan bread on a baking tray and sprinkle the edges with water.

2 Spread the ketchup and mustard over the bread, then slice the onion or shallots, mushrooms and tomato and scatter over the top. Season to taste, then place the sausages and bacon on top of the vegetables.

3 Bake in the oven, preheated to 200°C/400°F/gas mark 6, for 15 minutes or until the sausages are cooked through.

Preparation time: 10 minutes
Cooking time: 15 minutes

ALL-IN-ONE BREAKFAST BAPS

Serves 1

Ingredients	Metric	Imperial	American
Vegetable oil	15 ml	1 tbsp	1 tbsp
Sausages	2	2	2
Bacon rashers (slices), rinded	2	2	2
Mashed potato	60 ml	4 tbsp	4 tbsp
Floury white baps	2	2	2
Butter or margarine	10 ml	2 tsp	2 tsp
Tomato ketchup (catsup)	10 ml	2 tsp	2 tsp
Salt and freshly ground black pepper			

1 Heat the oil in a frying pan (skillet) and fry (sauté) the sausages and bacon for 5 minutes. Add the potato to the pan and cook until heated through.

2 Slice each bap in half and spread with the butter or margarine and ketchup.

3 Cut the sausages in half lengthways, then divide all the ingredients between the baps. Season to taste and serve.

Preparation time: 2 minutes
Cooking time: 10 minutes

BREAKFAST OMELETTE

Serves 1

Ingredients	Metric	Imperial	American
Vegetable oil	15 ml	1 tbsp	1 tbsp
Sausage, sliced	1	1	1
Bacon rasher (slice), rinded and chopped	1	1	1
Mushrooms, sliced	3	3	3
Tomato, sliced	1	1	1
Cooked potato, sliced	1	1	1
Salt and freshly ground black pepper			
Eggs, beaten	2	2	2

1 Heat the oil in a 15–20 cm/6–8 in frying pan (skillet), add the sausage slices and cook for 2 minutes. Add the bacon and cook for another 2 minutes.

2 Add the sliced mushrooms, tomato and potato and cook for 5 minutes, stirring occasionally. Season well with salt and pepper.

3 Pour over the beaten egg and cook over a gentle heat for a few minutes until the egg is set. Serve immediately.

 Preparation time: 5 minutes
Cooking time: 15 minutes

TIP: Buy a packet of bacon bits at the supermarket – they're cheaper and you don't need to chop them up!

POTATO CAKES WITH FRIED EGGS

Serves 1

Ingredients	Metric	Imperial	American
Mashed potato	90 ml	6 tbsp	6 tbsp
Onion, chopped	½	½	½
OR Shallots, chopped	1–2	1–2	1–2
Plain (all-purpose) flour	15 ml	1 tbsp	1 tbsp
Milk	30 ml	2 tbsp	2 tbsp
Vegetable oil	30 ml	2 tbsp	2 tbsp
Eggs	2	2	2

Salt and freshly ground black pepper

1   Mix together the potato, onion or shallots, flour and milk. Using lightly floured hands, pat the mixture into two even-sized rounds.

2   Heat half the vegetable oil in a large frying pan (skillet) and cook the potato cakes for 5–8 minutes on one side until brown and crisp. Turn them over to cook the second side.

3   While they are cooking, heat the remaining oil in the pan and break the eggs into the pan (push the potato cakes out of the way first). Fry (sauté) the eggs until cooked to your liking.

4   Remove the cakes from the pan, top each with an egg, season to taste and serve.

>)) Preparation time: 5 minutes
Cooking time: 20 minutes

SAUSAGE CROQUE MONSIEUR

**This sounds posh but it's basically a variation on a
traditional French fried (sautéed) sandwich!**

Serves 1

Ingredients	Metric	Imperial	American
Slices of bread	2	2	2
Butter or margarine	10 ml	2 tsp	2 tsp
Cheddar cheese, grated	30 ml	2 tbsp	2 tbsp
Sausages, cooked and sliced	2	2	2
Tomato ketchup (catsup) or made mustard	5 ml	1 tsp	1 tsp
Salt and freshly ground black pepper			

1 **Spread one side of each slice of bread with butter or
margarine. With the buttered sides out, make a
sandwich with the cheese, sausage, ketchup or mustard
and a little seasoning. Press the edges together.**

2 **Heat a frying pan (skillet) over a medium heat and
carefully slide the sandwich into the pan. Cook for a
couple of minutes on each side until the bread is
golden brown. Serve immediately.**

 **Preparation time: 5 minutes
Cooking time: 5 minutes**

CHEESY SAUSAGE SCRAMBLE ROLLS

Serves 1

Ingredients	Metric	Imperial	American
Eggs	2	2	2
Milk	30 ml	2 tbsp	2 tbsp
Salt and freshly ground black pepper			
Butter or margarine	10 ml	2 tsp	2 tsp
Cheese, grated	45 ml	3 tbsp	3 tbsp
Frankfurters, sliced	2	2	2
Soft white rolls	2	2	2

1 **Whisk together the eggs and milk using a fork. Season with salt and pepper.**

2 **Melt the butter or margarine in a small pan, add the egg and milk mixture and stir slowly over a gentle heat.**

3 **When the egg is almost cooked, stir in the cheese and the frankfurters and heat through.**

4 **Split the rolls in half, fill with the scramble mixture and serve immediately.**

Preparation time: 2 minutes
Cooking time: 5 minutes

SNACKS, SANDWICHES AND SALADS

FEED ME

You've had beans on toast three times already this week but you want something quick, tasty and a bit different, so read on ...

BEAN PATE

Serves 2–4

Ingredients	Metric	Imperial	American
Vegetable oil	15 ml	1 tbsp	1 tbsp
Onion, chopped	1	1	1
Garlic cloves, crushed	2	2	2
Peanut butter	15 ml	1 tbsp	1 tbsp
Lemon juice	30 ml	2 tbsp	2 tbsp
Chopped fresh parsley	30 ml	2 tbsp	2 tbsp
Can of butter (lima) beans, drained	400 g	14 oz	1 large

Hot buttered toast or chunks of raw carrot and (bell) peppers, to serve

1   Heat the oil in a medium pan, add the onion and garlic and fry (sauté) for 3–5 minutes until soft.

2   Add the remaining ingredients to the onion mixture and mash everything together with a fork. Spoon into a dish and chill in the fridge before serving with hot buttered toast or chunks of raw carrot and peppers.

Preparation time: 5 minutes
Cooking time: 5 minutes

SAUSAGE AND POTATO SALAD

Use smoked sausage for this main-course salad – you'll find it in the deli section of the supermarket.

Serves 2–3

Ingredients	Metric	Imperial	American
New potatoes, scrubbed	450 g	1 lb	1 lb
Smoked sausage, sliced	200 g	7 oz	7 oz
Cherry tomatoes, halved	10	10	10
Mayonnaise	60 ml	4 tbsp	4 tbsp
Wholegrain mustard	15 ml	1 tbsp	1 tbsp
Freshly ground black pepper			

1 Chop the potatoes into bite-sized pieces and cook in boiling salted water for 8–10 minutes or until tender. Drain, place in a bowl and leave to cool for 10 minutes.

2 Add the smoked sausage and the cherry tomatoes to the bowl. Mix together the mayonnaise and mustard and stir in to coat the other ingredients. Season with lots of black pepper.

Preparation time: 15 minutes
Cooking time: 10 minutes

TIP: For extra flavour, add some chopped fresh parsley or a few torn fresh basil leaves.

SPICY BEAN SALAD WITH FRENCH DRESSING

This is delicious with jacket potatoes. You can use almost any kind of bean – cannellini, red kidney and butter (lima) – and can vary the dressing by adding 30 ml/2 tbsp chopped fresh parsley or coriander (cilantro) or a crushed garlic clove.

Serves 4

Ingredients	Metric	Imperial	American
For the Spicy Bean Salad:			
Cans of beans of your choice, drained	2 × 400 g	2 × 14 oz	2 large
Red (bell) pepper, chopped	1	1	1
Green pepper, chopped	1	1	1
Red chilli, chopped	1	1	1
Salt and freshly ground black pepper			
For the French Dressing:			
White wine vinegar	15 ml	1 tbsp	1 tbsp
Olive oil	90 ml	6 tbsp	6 tbsp
Made mustard	5 ml	1 tsp	1 tsp
Salt and freshly ground black pepper			

1 Place all the ingredients for the Spicy Bean Salad in a large bowl, season well to taste, and stir to mix.

2 Combine all the ingredients for the French Dressing, add to the bowl and stir so that the beans are all well coated in the dressing.

Preparation time: 10 minutes
Cooking time: None

TIP: **Wash your hands very thoroughly after chopping a chilli – if you get even the tiniest amount of chilli juice in your eyes, by wiping them with your hand, you will soon know all about it!**

HOT SAUSAGE SANDWICH

Serves 1

Ingredients	Metric	Imperial	American
Herby pork sausages	2	2	2
Wholegrain mustard	5 ml	1 tsp	1 tsp
Plain yoghurt	15 ml	1 tbsp	1 tbsp
Thick slices of white crusty bread	2	2	2
Salad leaves and tomato slices, to serve			

1 **Grill (broil) the sausages under a preheated grill (broiler) for 10–15 minutes or until cooked.**

2 **Mix together the mustard and yoghurt. Place the cooked sausages on one slice of bread, drizzle the yoghurt mixture over, then add the salad leaves and tomato slices and top with the second slice of bread.**

Preparation time: 5 minutes
Cooking time: 15 minutes

SCOTCH RAREBIT

For a vegetarian option, top the egg mixture with green or red (bell) pepper slices or tomato slices, instead of the ham.

Serves 2

Ingredients	Metric	Imperial	American
Cheddar cheese, grated	225 g	8 oz	2 cups
Eggs, beaten	4	4	4
Salt and freshly ground black pepper			
Plain (all-purpose) flour	10 ml	2 tsp	2 tsp
Slices of bread	4	4	4
Cooked ham, diced	50 g	2 oz	½ cup

1 Mix together the cheese and eggs and season with salt and pepper. Stir in the flour.

2 Toast the slices of bread on one side. Spread the egg mixture on to the uncooked sides of the bread. Sprinkle with the ham and grill (broil) until golden.

 Preparation time: 5 minutes
 Cooking time: 10 minutes

TIP: For a stronger flavour, add a few drops of Tabasco sauce to the egg mixture or spread a thin layer of made mustard on the untoasted sides of the bread.

CHEESY SAUSAGE PITTAS

Pitta bread is a traditional Middle Eastern bread. Cut each
one in half and open to form two pockets ready to be
stuffed with any sandwich filling of your choice.

Serves 1

Ingredients	Metric	Imperial	American
Vegetable oil	15 ml	1 tbsp	1 tbsp
Sausages, sliced	2	2	2
Onion, sliced	½	½	½
OR Shallots, sliced	1–2	1–2	1–2
Red (bell) pepper, sliced	½	½	½
Pitta breads	2	2	2
Lettuce, shredded	45 ml	3 tbsp	3 tbsp
Cheddar cheese, grated	50 g	2 oz	½ cup

1 Heat the oil in a frying pan (skillet), add the sausage
slices and fry (sauté) for 5 minutes until lightly
browned.

2 Add the sliced onion or shallots and cook for
5 minutes. Add the sliced pepper and cook for
5 minutes.

3 Warm the pitta breads according to the packet
instructions. Fill the breads with the hot sausage filling
and top with lettuce and grated cheese.

Preparation time: 5 minutes
Cooking time: 15 minutes

PIZZA ROLLS

You can top these pizza rolls with lots of different
ingredients – try cooked bacon or tuna instead of the
salami, or add (bell) peppers or mushrooms to the pan
with the onions.

Serves 2

Ingredients	Metric	Imperial	American
Vegetable oil	15 ml	1 tbsp	1 tbsp
Onion, chopped	½	½	½
OR Shallots, chopped	1–2	1–2	1–2
Large white rolls, halved	2	2	2
Tomatoes, sliced	2	2	2
Salami slices	50 g	2 oz	2 oz
Cheese, grated	60 ml	4 tbsp	4 tbsp
Freshly ground black pepper			

1 Heat the vegetable oil in a small pan, add the chopped
   onion or shallots and cook gently for 5 minutes until
   soft.

2 Spread the onion or shallots evenly over the halved
   rolls, top with the tomato slices and grill (broil) for
   5 minutes.

3 Arrange the salami slices on top of the tomato and top
   with the cheese. Grill for a few minutes or until the
   cheese is golden brown and bubbling. Sprinkle with
   black pepper before serving.

Preparation time: 5 minutes
Cooking time: 10 minutes

PASTA AND SMOKED SAUSAGE SALAD

Serves 2

Ingredients	Metric	Imperial	American
Pasta shapes	175 g	6 oz	6 oz
Red (bell) pepper, diced	½	½	½
Green pepper, diced	½	½	½
Smoked sausage, sliced	75 g	3 oz	3 oz
Spring onions (scallions), sliced	2	2	2
Plain yoghurt	75 ml	5 tbsp	5 tbsp
Lemon juice	15 ml	1 tbsp	1 tbsp
Crusty bread, to serve			

1 Cook the pasta shapes according to the packet instructions. Drain, rinse in cold water and drain again.

2 Put the cooked pasta in a serving dish and stir in all the remaining ingredients. Season to taste and serve with crusty bread.

 Preparation time: 5 minutes
Cooking time: 10 minutes

TIP: Add any of the following to this basic recipe for a change:
  5 ml/1 tsp wholegrain mustard
  50 g/2 oz/½ cup cubed cheese
  6 halved cherry tomatoes
  15 ml/1 tbsp chopped fresh parsley
  50 g/2 oz/½ cup cooked mushrooms

BAKED BEAN AND SAUSAGE WRAPS

Look for sandwich wraps in the bread section in larger supermarkets – they're like flour tortillas but bigger. If you can't find sandwich wraps, this filling works just as well in pitta bread or toasted sandwiches.

Serves 1

Ingredients	Metric	Imperial	American
Sausages, cooked and sliced	2	2	2
Baked beans in tomato sauce	60 ml	4 tbsp	4 tbsp
Sandwich wraps	2	2	2
Grated cheese	30 ml	2 tbsp	2 tbsp

1 Put the sausage slices and baked beans in a small pan and heat gently until warmed through.

2 Spoon half the mixture into the centre of each wrap and top with the cheese. Fold the opposite sides together and then tuck the ends in to make a neat parcel.

3 Place on a baking (cookie) tray and warm through in a preheated oven at 190°C/375°F/gas mark 5 for 5–10 minutes.

Preparation time: 5 minutes
Cooking time: 5–10 minutes

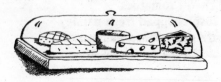

FALAFELS

These are traditional vegetarian patties from the Middle East. Serve them in pitta bread with salad, accompanied by a simple, creamy dressing made from plain yoghurt and chopped cucumber, seasoned with salt and freshly ground black pepper.

Serves 4

Ingredients	Metric	Imperial	American
Can of chick peas (garbanzos), drained	400 g	14 oz	1 large
Garlic cloves, crushed	4	4	4
Ground coriander (cilantro)	10 ml	2 tsp	2 tsp
Ground cumin	10 ml	2 tsp	2 tsp
Onion, chopped	1	1	1
Plain (all-purpose) flour	15 ml	1 tbsp	1 tbsp
Chopped fresh parsley	30 ml	2 tbsp	2 tbsp
A little vegetable oil			

1 Mash the chick peas with a potato masher or a fork until smooth. Season well and add the remaining ingredients except the oil.

2 Shape the mixture into small rounds about 6 cm/2½ in across. Pour about 1 cm/½ in vegetable oil into a frying pan (skillet) and heat it. Place a crumb of the mixture into the pan and when it begins to sizzle the oil is ready to cook. Fry (sauté) the falafels for 2–3 minutes on each side until golden brown.

 Preparation time: 5 minutes
Cooking time: 10 minutes

SPICY CHICK PEA DIP

Serve this with warm pitta bread and chunks of raw (bell) pepper and carrot, or spread it on wholemeal bread with slices of tomato and cucumber for a tasty veggie sandwich.

Serves 4

Ingredients	Metric	Imperial	American
Vegetable oil	15 ml	1 tbsp	1 tbsp
Onion, chopped	1	1	1
Clove of garlic, crushed	1	1	1
Can of chick peas (garbanzos), drained	400 g	14 oz	1 large
Lemon juice	30 ml	2 tbsp	2 tbsp
Ground cumin	5 ml	1 tsp	1 tsp
Chilli powder	2.5 ml	½ tsp	½ tsp
Plain yoghurt	30 ml	2 tbsp	2 tbsp

1 Heat the oil in a small pan, add the onion and garlic and fry (sauté) for 5 minutes.

2 Mash the chick peas with a potato masher or fork until smooth. Stir the onion and garlic into the chick peas, add the remaining ingredients, season and stir well. Spoon into a serving dish and chill in the fridge.

Preparation time: 5 minutes
Cooking time: 5 minutes

CURRIED EGG MAYONNAISE

This makes a delicious filling for sandwiches or a topping for baked potatoes.

Serves 2

Ingredients	Metric	Imperial	American
Eggs	4	4	4
Mayonnaise	75 ml	5 tbsp	5 tbsp
Curry powder	10 ml	2 tsp	2 tsp
Salt and freshly ground black pepper			

1 To hard-boil (hard-cook) the eggs, bring a pan of water to the boil and add the eggs. Reduce the heat and simmer for 6–7 minutes. As soon as the time is up, place the eggs under cold running water to cool them quickly.

2 Mix together the mayonnaise and curry powder in a small bowl. Remove the shells from the cooled eggs. Chop the eggs into small pieces, stir into the curry mayonnaise and season to taste with salt and pepper.

 Preparation time: 5 minutes
Cooking time: 6–7 minutes

SAUSAGE DIPPERS

Serves 4

Ingredients	Metric	Imperial	American
Skinless sausages	8	8	8
Streaky bacon rashers (slices), rinded and halved lengthways	4	4	4
Cheddar cheese, cut into 8 strips as long as the sausages	100 g	4 oz	1 cup
Ready-made spicy tomato dip, to serve			

1 Cut a slit lengthways in each sausage. Place a strip of cheese into each sausage and wrap a piece of bacon around each one.

2 Cook under a preheated grill (broiler) for about 10 minutes or until the bacon is crisp and the sausages are cooked through. Serve with spicy tomato dip.

Preparation time: 5 minutes
Cooking time: 10 minutes

STUFFED SAUSAGE BAGUETTE

Serves 1

Ingredients	Metric	Imperial	American
Vegetable oil	15 ml	1 tbsp	1 tbsp
Sausages	2	2	2
Onion, sliced	½	½	½
OR Shallots, sliced	1–2	1–2	1–2
Small baguette	1	1	1
Butter or margarine	10 ml	2 tsp	2 tsp
Tomato ketchup (catsup)	5 ml	1 tsp	1 tsp
Wholegrain mustard	2.5 ml	½ tsp	½ tsp

1 **Heat the vegetable oil in a small pan, add the sausages and fry (sauté) for 5 minutes. Add the sliced onion or shallot to the pan and cook for 5 minutes or until it is browned and the sausages are cooked.**

2 **Slice the baguette in half horizontally, spread with the butter or margarine, ketchup and mustard, and fill with the cooked sausages and onions.**

»》 **Preparation time: 5 minutes**
Cooking time: 10 minutes

VEGGIE BURGERS

**You can add any diced vegetables to the mixture –
try carrots, celery, leeks or courgettes (zucchini) instead
of the (bell) peppers.**

Serves 3

Ingredients	Metric	Imperial	American
Vegetable oil	45 ml	3 tbsp	3 tbsp
Onion, chopped	1	1	1
Garlic clove, crushed	1	1	1
Red pepper, diced	½	½	½
Green pepper, diced	½	½	½
Can of butter (lima) beans, drained	400 g	14 oz	1 large
Chilli powder	2.5 ml	½ tsp	½ tsp
Dried parsley	5 ml	1 tsp	1 tsp
Salt and freshly ground black pepper			
Plain (all-purpose) flour	30 ml	2 tbsp	2 tbsp
Burger buns, split in half	6	6	6
Cheese slices	6	6	6
Tomato slices, mayonnaise, sweetcorn (corn) relish and tomato ketchup (catsup), to serve			

1 **Heat 15 ml/1 tbsp of the oil in a frying pan (skillet) and cook the onion for 3 minutes until soft. Add the garlic and peppers to the pan and cook for 5 minutes.**

2 **In a small mixing bowl, mash the butter beans with a fork or potato masher to a smooth paste. Stir in the fried (sautéed) vegetables, chilli powder, parsley and salt and pepper.**

3 Using your hands divide the mixture into six even-sized burgers. Coat each burger in flour.

4 Heat the remaining oil in the frying pan and cook the burgers over a medium heat for 5 minutes on each side.

5 While the burgers are cooking, place a slice of cheese on the bottom halves of the buns and toast until the cheese is golden and bubbling. Top each bun with a burger, tomato slices and mayonnaise, relish and ketchup, then place the other halves of the buns on top.

 Preparation time: 15 minutes
Cooking time: 10–15 minutes

TIP: For nutty bean burgers, add 30 ml/2 tbsp chopped mixed nuts to the mashed bean mixture.

ONE-POT DINNERS

FEED ME

Everyone (especially students!) hates washing up, so if you can try and make your main course in one pan it makes life a lot easier. Some of the recipes in this chapter show you how to make entire meals in one pan; others can be served with simple accompaniments such as rice or pasta, which generate a minimum of dirty pans, and jacket potatoes and crusty bread, which make none at all!

SAUSAGE AND BEAN BAKE

**Pop a couple of jacket potatoes in the oven first and they
should be ready at the same time as the bake.**

Serves 2

Ingredients	Metric	Imperial	American
Vegetable oil	15 ml	1 tbsp	1 tbsp
Onion, chopped	1	1	1
Garlic clove, crushed	1	1	1
Can of tomatoes, chopped	400 g	14 oz	1 large
Can of butter (lima) beans, drained	400 g	14 oz	1 large
Can of cannellini beans, drained	400 g	14 oz	1 large
Pork or vegetarian sausages	4	4	4
Dried sage	5 ml	1 tsp	1 tsp
Salt and freshly ground black pepper			
Crusty bread or jacket potatoes, to serve			

1 Heat the oil in a flameproof casserole dish (Dutch
oven), add the onion and garlic and fry (sauté) over
a medium heat for 3–5 minutes until soft. Add the
tomatoes and beans, stir well and cook for a further
5 minutes.

2 Add the sausages to the casserole, sprinkle with the
sage and season with salt and pepper.

3 Cover and cook in a preheated oven at 180°C/350°F/
gas mark 4 for 1 hour. Serve with crusty bread or
jacket potatoes.

**Preparation time: 10 minutes
Cooking time: 1 hour**

POTATO AND CHICK PEA CURRY

This simple curry is quick to make – and you don't even need to peel the potatoes!

Serves 3–4

Ingredients	Metric	Imperial	American
Medium potatoes, unpeeled but scrubbed	3	3	3
Salt			
Vegetable oil	30 ml	2 tbsp	2 tbsp
Onion, chopped	1	1	1
Garlic clove, crushed	1	1	1
Green (bell) pepper, chopped	1	1	1
Can of tomatoes, chopped	400 g	14 oz	1 large
Mild curry powder	45 ml	3 tbsp	3 tbsp
Can of chick peas (garbanzos), drained	400 g	14 oz	1 large
Boiled rice or naan bread, to serve			

1 Chop the potatoes into bite-sized chunks and cook in boiling salted water for 10 minutes. Drain.

2 While the potatoes are cooking, heat the vegetable oil in a frying pan (skillet) and fry (sauté) the onion and garlic for 3–5 minutes. Add the drained potatoes and the pepper and cook for 5 minutes, stirring occasionally.

3 Add the remaining ingredients and cook the curry gently for 10 minutes. If the mixture seems too thick, add a little water and heat through before serving with boiled rice or naan bread.

 Preparation time: 15 minutes
Cooking time: 10 minutes

TIP: Naan bread is a traditional Indian flat bread, usually served warm. To heat the bread, either grill (broil) or bake according to the packet instructions. Look out for flavoured naan bread in the supermarket – garlic and coriander (cilantro) goes well with this curry.

PEPPER AND SAUSAGE STIR-FRY

Serves 2

Ingredients	Metric	Imperial	American
Vegetable oil	30 ml	2 tbsp	2 tbsp
Onion, sliced	1	1	1
Sausages	4	4	4
Red (bell) pepper, sliced	1	1	1
Yellow pepper, sliced	1	1	1
Clear honey	30 ml	2 tbsp	2 tbsp
Made mustard	15 ml	1 tbsp	1 tbsp
Boiled rice or pitta bread, to serve			

1   Heat the vegetable oil in a frying pan (skillet), add the onion and sausages and fry (sauté) for 3–5 minutes until the sausages are lightly browned.

2   Add the peppers, honey and mustard and cook for 5–10 minutes until the sausages are cooked right through.

3   Serve with boiled rice or warm pitta bread.

Preparation time: 10 minutes
Cooking time: 10 minutes

SAUSAGE JAMBALAYA

Serves 2

Ingredients	Metric	Imperial	American
Vegetable oil	60 ml	4 tbsp	4 tbsp
Onion, sliced	1	1	1
Garlic cloves, crushed	3	3	3
Celery sticks, sliced	2	2	2
White rice	225 g	8 oz	1 cup
Dried thyme	5 ml	1 tsp	1 tsp
Can of tomatoes, chopped	400 g	14 oz	1 large
Sugar	2.5 ml	½ tsp	½ tsp
Chicken stock	450 ml	¾ pt	2 cups
A few drops of Tabasco sauce			
Red (bell) pepper, sliced	1	1	1
Smoked sausage, sliced	225 g	8 oz	8 oz
Salt and freshly ground black pepper			

1 Heat the oil in a large pan, add the onion, garlic and celery and fry (sauté) for 3 minutes, stirring constantly. Add the rice and cook for 1 minute.

2 Add the thyme, tomatoes, sugar, stock and Tabasco sauce and bring to the boil. Reduce the heat, cover and cook gently for 10 minutes or until the rice is tender and the stock has been absorbed.

3 Stir in the sliced pepper and sausage, season with salt and pepper and stir until heated through.

Preparation time: 10 minutes
Cooking time: 15 minutes

VEGGIE CHILLI

Quorn is a meat substitute, made from myco protein from mushrooms. It's lower in fat than beef and meat-eaters won't be able to tell the difference!

Serves 2–3

Ingredients	Metric	Imperial	American
Vegetable oil	15 ml	1 tbsp	1 tbsp
Onion, chopped	1	1	1
Garlic cloves, crushed	2	2	2
Minced (ground) Quorn	225 g	8 oz	8 oz
Chilli powder	10 ml	2 tsp	2 tsp
Can of tomatoes, chopped	400 g	14 oz	1 large
Can of kidney beans, drained	400 g	14 oz	1 large
Green (bell) pepper, chopped	1	1	1
Red pepper, chopped	1	1	1
Boiled rice, plain yoghurt and grated cheese, to serve			

1   Heat the oil in a large saucepan, add the onion and garlic and stir-fry for 3–5 minutes. Add the Quorn and chilli powder and stir-fry for 3 minutes.

2   Add the remaining ingredients and stir well. Cover and cook over a gentle heat for 20–30 minutes, stirring occasionally.

3   Serve on a bed of boiled rice with a dollop of plain yoghurt and plenty of grated cheese.

Preparation time: 10 minutes
Cooking time: 30 minutes

CHILLI BEAN CASSEROLE

**This warming spicy dish goes well with jacket potatoes
(cook them in the oven at the same time) or rice.**

Serves 2

Ingredients	Metric	Imperial	American
Vegetable oil	15 ml	1 tbsp	1 tbsp
Onion, chopped	1	1	1
Courgette (zucchini), sliced	1	1	1
Can of tomatoes, chopped	400 g	14 oz	1 large
Can of kidney beans, drained	400 g	14 oz	1 large
Chilli powder	10 ml	2 tsp	2 tsp
Dried sage	5 ml	1 tsp	1 tsp

1   Heat the oil in a flameproof casserole (Dutch oven),
add the onion and fry (sauté) for 3–5 minutes. Add
the courgette and fry for 2 minutes.

2   Add the remaining ingredients, stir well and cook
in a preheated oven at 190°C/375°F/gas mark 5
for 50 minutes.

**» Preparation time: 10 minutes
Cooking time: 50 minutes**

WINTER VEGETABLE STEW WITH CHEESE DUMPLINGS

There's a long list of ingredients for this dish, but it makes a real treat on a cold winter's day.

Serves 3–4

Ingredients	Metric	Imperial	American
Butter or margarine	50 g	2 oz	¼ cup
Leeks, sliced	2	2	2
Parsnips, sliced	2	2	2
Carrots, sliced	2	2	2
Potatoes, cubed	2	2	2
Plain (all-purpose) flour	200 g	7 oz	1¾ cups
Baking powder	10 ml	2 tsp	2 tsp
Salt	5 ml	1 tsp	1 tsp
Grated Cheddar cheese	60 ml	4 tbsp	4 tbsp
Egg, beaten	1	1	1
Milk	100 ml	3½ fl oz	scant ½ cup
Vegetable stock	900 ml	1½ pts	3¾ cups
Dried parsley	5 ml	1 tsp	1 tsp
Dried thyme	5ml	1 tsp	1 tsp
Can of flageolet beans, drained	400 g	14 oz	1 large

1 Melt the butter or margarine in a large pan, add the leeks, parsnips, carrots and potatoes and stir well. Cover and cook over a medium heat for 30 minutes, stirring occasionally.

2 To make the dumplings, place the flour, baking powder, salt and cheese in a bowl. Add the egg and just enough milk to make a soft dough. Form into eight or nine even-sized balls.

3 Add the stock, herbs and beans to the vegetables, bring to the boil and cook for 10 minutes.

4 Put the dumplings on top of the stew, cover and simmer for 10–15 minutes until everything is cooked through.

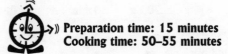

)) Preparation time: 15 minutes
Cooking time: 50–55 minutes

TIP: Any root vegetables work well in this stew – try swede (rutabaga), turnip or celery.

BOOZY SAUSAGE AND APPLE CASSEROLE

Lager, sausages and apples may sound like an odd combination but this really tastes great!

Serves 2

Ingredients	Metric	Imperial	American
Vegetable oil	60 ml	4 tbsp	4 tbsp
Sausages	4	4	4
Potatoes, sliced	700 g	1½ lb	1½ lb
Eating (dessert) apples, sliced	2	2	2
Salt and freshly ground black pepper			
Lager	200 ml	7 fl oz	scant 1 cup
Cheese, grated	45 ml	3 tbsp	3 tbsp

1 Heat 30 ml/2 tbsp of the oil in a flameproof casserole (Dutch oven) and fry (sauté) the sausages until browned. Remove from the casserole dish and chop into chunks.

2 Heat the remaining oil in the casserole and fry the potato slices for 5 minutes.

3 Add the apple slices to the pan, season well with salt and pepper and pour over the lager. Add the sausage chunks to the pan and stir well. Sprinkle over the cheese, cover and bake at 190°C/375°/gas mark 5 for 50 minutes or until the potatoes are cooked.

Preparation time: 10 minutes
Cooking time: 50 minutes

SWEET AND SOUR SAUSAGES

Serves 2

Ingredients	Metric	Imperial	American
Vegetable oil	15 ml	1 tbsp	1 tbsp
Pork sausages	4	4	4
Onion, chopped	1	1	1
Can of pineapple chunks	200 g	7 oz	1 small
Tomato purée (paste)	30 ml	2 tbsp	2 tbsp
White wine vinegar	45 ml	3 tbsp	3 tbsp
Soy sauce	45 ml	3 tbsp	3 tbsp
Water	150 ml	¼ pt	⅔ cup
Red (bell) pepper, diced	½	½	½
Green pepper, diced	½	½	½
Cornflour (cornstarch)	15 ml	1 tbsp	1 tbsp
Boiled rice, to serve			

1 Heat the oil in a frying pan (skillet), add the sausages and onion and cook gently for 5 minutes.

2 Add the pineapple chunks and their juice to the pan and stir well. Add the tomato purée, wine vinegar and soy sauce and stir well. Add the water and pepper and bring to the boil.

3 Meanwhile, in a mug, blend the cornflour with 45 ml/ 3 tbsp cold water to make a paste. Add the cornflour mixture to the pan and stir well. Turn down the heat and cook for 20 minutes. Serve with boiled rice.

Preparation time: 10 minutes
Cooking time: 20 minutes

SAUSAGES WITH SPICY TOMATO SAUCE

Serves 2

Ingredients	Metric	Imperial	American
Vegetable oil	15 ml	1 tbsp	1 tbsp
Onion, chopped	1	1	1
Garlic cloves, crushed	2	2	2
Can of tomatoes, chopped	400 g	14 oz	1 large
Chilli powder	10 ml	2 tsp	2 tsp
Sausages	4	4	4
Crusty bread, to serve			

1 Heat the oil in a saucepan and cook the onion and garlic for 5 minutes until soft.

2 Add the tomatoes and chilli powder and cook for 15 minutes.

3 While the sauce is cooking, cook the sausages under a preheated grill (broiler) for 10–15 minutes or until browned and cooked through.

4 Pour the sauce over the sausages and serve with lots of crusty bread to soak up the sauce.

Preparation time: 5 minutes
Cooking time: 15 minutes

PORK AND BEAN STEW

Serves 4

Ingredients	Metric	Imperial	American
Vegetable oil	30 ml	2 tbsp	2 tbsp
Stewing pork, cubed	450 g	1 lb	1 lb
Garlic clove, crushed	1	1	1
Leek, sliced	1	1	1
Parsnips, sliced	2	2	2
Dried sage	5 ml	1 tsp	1 tsp
Apple juice	300 ml	½ pt	1¼ cups
Can of cannellini beans, drained	400 g	14 oz	1 large
Water	300 ml	½ pt	1¼ cups
Salt and freshly ground black pepper			
Boiled brown rice, to serve			

1   **Heat half the oil in an ovenproof casserole (Dutch oven) and fry (sauté) the pork until browned. Remove from the dish and place on a plate.**

2   **Fry the garlic, leek and parsnips in the remaining oil in the dish. Return the pork to the pan and add all the remaining ingredients, seasoning well with salt and pepper.**

3   **Bring the stew to the boil and cover. Cook in a preheated oven at 160°C/325°F/gas mark 3 for 1½ hours or until tender.**

4   **Serve with boiled brown rice.**

Preparation time: 10 minutes
Cooking time: 1½ hours

SAUSAGE AND LENTIL CASSEROLE

There are so many different types of sausages available –
just use your favourites in this recipe. Pork and bacon
sausages work particularly well.

Serves 4

Ingredients	Metric	Imperial	American
Vegetable oil	15 ml	1 tbsp	1 tbsp
Pork and leek sausages	8	8	8
Bacon rashers (slices), rinded and chopped	8	8	8
Onion, chopped	1	1	1
Garlic clove, crushed	1	1	1
Carrot, sliced	1	1	1
Swede (rutabaga), cubed	½	½	½
Red lentils	25 g	1 oz	3 tbsp
Vegetable stock	600 ml	1 pt	2½ cups
Tomato purée (paste)	30 ml	2 tbsp	2 tbsp
Worcestershire sauce	30 ml	2 tbsp	2 tbsp
Crusty bread, to serve			

1   Heat the oil in a large frying pan (skillet) and fry
    (sauté) the sausages and bacon for 4–5 minutes until
    lightly browned.

2   Cut the sausages in half. Add the onion and garlic to
    the frying pan and cook gently for 2 minutes.

3   Add all the remaining ingredients and season well.
Bring to the boil, then turn down the heat and simmer
for 25–30 minutes until the vegetables are cooked.
Add a little water if the casserole seems too dry.

4   Serve with crusty bread.

Preparation time: 10 minutes
Cooking time: 30 minutes

CHEESY LEEK AND SAUSAGE BAKE

Serve this dish with jacket potatoes – put them in the oven about 40 minutes before you start making the bake.

Serves 2

Ingredients	Metric	Imperial	American
Vegetable oil	15 ml	1 tbsp	1 tbsp
Leeks, sliced	2	2	2
Canned frankfurters	6	6	6
Cheese sauce (see page 19)	300 ml	½ pt	1¼ cups
Mustard powder	5 ml	1 tsp	1 tsp
Salt and freshly ground black pepper			
Cheddar cheese, grated	50 g	2 oz	½ cup

1 Heat the vegetable oil in an ovenproof casserole (Dutch oven) and gently fry (sauté) the leeks for 3–5 minutes.

2 Chop the frankfurters into bite-sized chunks and add to the leeks.

3 Pour the cheese sauce over the mixture and sprinkle with the mustard powder. Season with salt and pepper and stir well to coat the leeks and frankfurters with the sauce.

4 Top with the grated cheese and bake in a preheated oven for 20 minutes at 190°C/375°F/gas mark 5 or until the cheese has turned golden brown.

Preparation time: 10 minutes
Cooking time: 20 minutes

TIP: For convenience, buy ready-made sauce in a carton.

CHILLI CON CARNE

This is a classic dish – serve it with rice, use it to fill flour tortillas or simply top with grated cheese and scoop it up with nachos.

Serves 4

Ingredients	Metric	Imperial	American
Vegetable oil	30 ml	2 tbsp	2 tbsp
Onion, chopped	1	1	1
Garlic cloves, crushed	2	2	2
Minced (ground) beef	450 g	1 lb	1 lb
Can of tomatoes, chopped	400 g	14 oz	1 large
Can of red kidney beans, drained	400 g	14 oz	1 large
Chilli powder	10 ml	2 tsp	2 tsp
Beef stock	150 ml	¼ pt	⅔ cup
Tomato purée (paste)	15 ml	1 tbsp	1 tbsp
Salt and freshly ground black pepper			

1 **Heat the oil in a saucepan, add the onion and garlic and fry (sauté) for 3–5 minutes.**

2 **Add the minced beef and stir until browned.**

3 **Add all the remaining ingredients, bring to the boil, then reduce the heat, cover and simmer gently for 30–35 minutes, stirring occasionally, until cooked through. Season to taste with salt and pepper.**

Preparation time: 10 minutes
Cooking time: 35 minutes

ORIENTAL STIR-FRY

Serves 2

Ingredients	Metric	Imperial	American
Medium egg noodles	250 g	9 oz	9 oz
Vegetable oil	15 ml	1 tbsp	1 tbsp
Onion, sliced	1	1	1
Garlic clove, crushed	1	1	1
Carrot, cut into strips	1	1	1
Red (bell) pepper, sliced	1	1	1
Beansprouts	100 g	4 oz	4 oz
Smoked sausage, sliced	100 g	4 oz	4 oz
Soy sauce	30 ml	2 tbsp	2 tbsp
Clear honey	30 ml	2 tbsp	2 tbsp
Ground ginger	10 ml	2 tsp	2 tsp

1 Cook the noodles according to the packet instructions, then drain well.

2 Heat the oil in a large frying pan (skillet) and fry (sauté) the onion for 3 minutes until soft.

3 Add the garlic and carrot and stir-fry for 3 minutes. Add the pepper and cook for 1 minute. Add the beansprouts and cook for 2 minutes. Add the remaining ingredients and the noodles and stir-fry for 2 minutes or until the noodles are heated through.

Preparation time: 10 minutes
Cooking time: 10 minutes

TIP: For a genuine oriental flavour, sprinkle the noodles with 15 ml/1 tbsp sesame oil just before serving.

SAUSAGE AND LEEK TORTILLA

Serves 2

Ingredients	Metric	Imperial	American
Vegetable oil	15 ml	1 tbsp	1 tbsp
Potatoes, cooked and chopped into bite-sized pieces	225 g	8 oz	8 oz
Leeks, sliced	2	2	2
Sausages, cooked and sliced	4	4	4
Eggs, beaten	3	3	3
Salt and freshly ground black pepper			
Grated Cheddar cheese	60 ml	4 tbsp	4 tbsp
Salad and crusty bread, to serve			

1 **Heat the oil in a frying pan (skillet) and fry (sauté) the potatoes and leeks for about 5 minutes until softened. Add the sausage slices to the pan.**

2 **Season the beaten eggs with salt and pepper and pour into the pan. Cook gently until the egg mixture is set on the base.**

3 **Sprinkle the cheese over the tortilla and grill (broil) under a preheated grill (broiler) until the cheese is golden brown.**

4 **Serve with salad and crusty bread.**

 **Preparation time: 5 minutes
Cooking time: 10 minutes**

RICE AND PASTA MAIN MEALS

FEED ME

They're cheap, they're easy to cook, they fill you up and they're great for when you've got a few friends coming round – so reach for the rice or pasta. Oh, and they're delicious too!

BEAN AND TOMATO SAUCE

This easy, filling sauce goes well with pasta, rice or sausages. Use whatever beans you have in the storecupboard – butter (lima), cannellini and borlotti all work well.

Serves 2–3

Ingredients	Metric	Imperial	American
Vegetable oil	15 ml	1 tbsp	1 tbsp
Onion, chopped	1	1	1
Garlic cloves, crushed	2	2	2
Can of tomatoes, chopped	400 g	14 oz	1 large
Dried basil	5 ml	1 tsp	1 tsp
Can of beans, drained	400 g	14 oz	1 large

1 Heat the oil in a medium pan, add the onion and garlic and cook gently for 3–5 minutes until soft.

2 Add all the remaining ingredients and cook for 15–20 minutes over a low heat, stirring occasionally until thickened.

Preparation time: 10 minutes
Cooking time: 20 minutes

VEGETABLE RISOTTO

It doesn't really matter what size of mug you use as long as you use the same one to measure both the rice and the water.

Serves 2

Ingredients	Metric	Imperial	American
Vegetable oil	15 ml	1 tbsp	1 tbsp
Onion, chopped	1	1	1
Garlic cloves, crushed	2	2	2
Brown rice	2 mugs	2 mugs	2 mugs
Boiling water	4 mugs	4 mugs	4 mugs
Can of red kidney beans, drained	400 g	14 oz	1 large
Chilli powder	5 ml	1 tsp	1 tsp
Soy sauce	15 ml	1 tbsp	1 tbsp
Dried thyme	5 ml	1 tsp	1 tsp
Red (bell) pepper, chopped	1	1	1
Yellow pepper, chopped	1	1	1
Frozen peas	½ mug	½ mug	½ mug
Can of sweetcorn (corn), drained	200 g	7 oz	1 medium
Salt and freshly ground black pepper			
Cheddar cheese, grated, to serve			

1 Heat the oil in a large frying pan (skillet), add the onion and garlic and fry (sauté) over a medium heat for 3–5 minutes.

2 Add the rice to the pan together with the water and stir well. Add the beans, chilli powder, soy sauce and thyme and bring to the boil. Stir well, reduce the heat to low and simmer gently for 20 minutes.

3 Add the remaining ingredients and cook for 10 minutes or until the rice is tender. Check the seasoning and serve with grated cheese sprinkled over the top.

Preparation time: 10 minutes
Cooking time: 35 minutes

TUNA AND BEAN PASTA BAKE

Tubular pasta works best in this recipe – try rigatoni (ribbed tubes) or penne (tubes with pointed ends) – the tuna and tomato sauce coats and fill the shapes.

Serves 2

Ingredients	Metric	Imperial	American
Pasta shapes	175 g	6 oz	6 oz
Vegetable oil	15 ml	1 tbsp	1 tbsp
Onion, chopped	1	1	1
Garlic clove, crushed	1	1	1
Can of tomatoes, chopped	400 g	14 oz	1 large
Dried basil	5 ml	1 tsp	1 tsp
Dried oregano	5 ml	1 tsp	1 tsp
Can of tuna in brine, drained	200 g	7 oz	1 small
Can of butter (lima) beans, drained	400 g	14 oz	1 large
Cheddar cheese, grated	100 g	4 oz	1 cup
Packet of plain crisps (chips), crushed	1 small	1 small	1 small

1 Cook the pasta in boiling water according to the packet instructions. Drain.

2 Meanwhile, heat the vegetable oil in a flameproof casserole (Dutch oven), add the onion and garlic and fry (sauté) over a medium heat for 3–5 minutes until soft.

3 Add the tomatoes, herbs, tuna and beans and stir well. Add the drained pasta, stirring to coat it with the sauce.

4 Top with the cheese and crisps and bake in a preheated oven at 180°C/350°F/gas mark 4 for 30–40 minutes until golden on top.

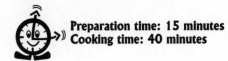

Preparation time: 15 minutes
Cooking time: 40 minutes

CHINESE-STYLE RICE

This dish is ideal for using up any leftover rice you have in the fridge. The mug size is not important. You can also add any leftover cooked, chopped meat – add with the sweetcorn and make sure it is heated through before serving.

Serves 2

Ingredients	Metric	Imperial	American
Vegetable oil	15 ml	1 tbsp	1 tbsp
Onion, chopped	1	1	1
Salt and freshly ground black pepper			
Red (bell) pepper, sliced	1	1	1
Green pepper, sliced	1	1	1
Eggs, beaten	2	2	2
White rice, cooked and cooled	3 mugs	3 mugs	3 mugs
Chilli powder	5 ml	1 tsp	1 tsp
Ground ginger	5 ml	1 tsp	1 tsp
Can of sweetcorn (corn), drained	200 g	7 oz	1 small

1 Heat the oil in a frying pan (skillet), until hot. Add the onion and salt and pepper and stir-fry for 2 minutes. Add the peppers and stir-fry for 1 minute. Add the beaten eggs and stir-fry for 1 minute.

2 Add the rice to the pan and stir-fry for 3 minutes. Add the chilli powder, ground ginger and sweetcorn and stir-fry for 5 minutes.

 Preparation time: 5 minutes
Cooking time: 15 minutes

CREAMY PASTA BAKE

Serves 2

Ingredients	Metric	Imperial	American
Pasta shapes	175 g	6 oz	6 oz
Vegetable oil	30 ml	2 tbsp	2 tbsp
Onion, chopped	1	1	1
Garlic clove, crushed	1	1	1
Single (light) cream	300 ml	½ pt	1¼ cups
Eggs, beaten	2	2	2
Salt and freshly ground black pepper			
Cheddar cheese, grated	100 g	4 oz	1 cup

1 Cook the pasta in boiling water according to the packet instructions. Drain and stir in 15 ml/1 tbsp vegetable oil.

2 Heat the remaining oil in a frying pan (skillet) and fry (sauté) the onion and garlic for 5 minutes until soft.

3 In a large ovenproof dish, mix together the cream and eggs and season with salt and pepper. Stir in the cheese, the onion mixture and the cooked pasta. Bake in a preheated oven at 190°C/375°F/gas mark 5 for 30–40 minutes until golden brown.

Preparation time: 10 minutes
Cooking time: 40 minutes

SPAGHETTI CARBONARA

Try to buy fresh Parmesan if you can – dried just doesn't taste the same. Buy it in a small block; it is expensive, but it keeps well in the fridge wrapped in clingfilm (plastic wrap) and can be grated and frozen.

Serves 1

Ingredients	Metric	Imperial	American
Spaghetti	100 g	4 oz	4 oz
Vegetable oil	15 ml	1 tbsp	1 tbsp
Bacon rashers (slices), rinded and chopped	2	2	2
Eggs	1	1	1
Parmesan cheese, grated	15 ml	1 tbsp	1 tbsp

Extra Parmesan cheese and freshly ground black pepper, to serve

1 **Cook the pasta in boiling water according to the packet instructions. Drain.**

2 **Meanwhile, heat the oil in a small frying pan (skillet) and fry (sauté) the chopped bacon until crisp.**

3 **Beat the eggs in a bowl and add the Parmesan.**

4 **When the pasta is cooked, drain it and return to the hot pan, quickly stir in the bacon and all the juices from the frying pan, and beat in the egg mixture, stirring until well combined.**

5 **Serve sprinkled with extra Parmesan and black pepper.**

Preparation time: 5 minutes
Cooking time: 10 minutes

TANGY SAUSAGES AND RICE

Serves 2

Ingredients	Metric	Imperial	American
Sausages	4	4	4
Garlic clove, halved	1	1	1
Clear honey	15 ml	1 tbsp	1 tbsp
Tomato purée (paste)	30 ml	2 tbsp	2 tbsp
Tabasco sauce	5 ml	1 tsp	1 tsp
Mustard powder	2.5 ml	½ tsp	½ tsp
Chicken stock	600 ml	1 pt	2½ cups
White rice	225 g	8 oz	1 cup
Raisins	100 g	4 oz	4 oz

1   Rub the sausages with the cut side of the garlic clove. Mix together the honey, tomato purée, Tabasco sauce and mustard powder.

2   Put the mixture in a casserole dish (Dutch oven) with the sausages and cover with about 45 ml/3 tbsp of the stock. Bake in a preheated oven at 190°C/375°F/gas mark 5 for 15 minutes.

3   Remove the sausages from the dish and add the remaining stock, the rice and raisins and stir well.

4   Arrange the sausages on top, cover with a lid or foil and bake for 45 minutes until the rice is tender and all the liquid has been absorbed.

 Preparation time: 20 minutes
Cooking time: 45 minutes

CHUNKY VEGETABLE PAPPARDELLE

Pappardelle is a wider version of tagliatelle, which will do just as well for this recipe.

Serves 2

Ingredients	Metric	Imperial	American
Vegetable oil	15 ml	1 tbsp	1 tbsp
Onion, chopped	1	1	1
Garlic clove, crushed	1	1	1
Courgette (zucchini), sliced	1	1	1
Can of tomatoes, chopped	400 g	14 oz	1 large
Can of butter (lima) beans, drained	400 g	14 oz	1 large
Green (bell) pepper, sliced	½	½	½
Bacon rashers (slices), rinded and chopped	3	3	3
Pappardelle	200 g	7oz	7 oz
Grated cheese, to serve			

1 Heat the oil in a large saucepan and fry (sauté) the onion and garlic for 5 minutes until soft.

2 Add all the remaining ingredients, except the bacon and pasta and cook for 15 minutes, stirring occasionally.

3 Meanwhile, grill (broil) the bacon until it is really crisp.

4 Cook the pasta in boiling water according to the packet instructions. Drain and serve topped with the sauce and the bacon.

Preparation time: 10 minutes
Cooking time: 20 minutes

CHEESY RIGATONI WITH LEEKS

Serves 2

Ingredients	Metric	Imperial	American
Rigatoni	175 g	6 oz	6 oz
Vegetable oil	15 ml	1 tbsp	1 tbsp
Leek, sliced	1	1	1
Cream cheese with garlic	250 g	9 oz	1 packet
Single (light) cream	150 ml	¼ pt	⅔ cup
Salt and freshly ground black pepper			
Frankfurters, cooked and sliced	4	4	4

1 Cook the rigatoni in boiling water according to the packet instructions. Drain.

2 Heat the oil in a large frying pan (skillet) and gently fry (sauté) the leek for 5 minutes. Reduce the heat to low, add the cream cheese to the pan and stir until the cheese melts.

3 Pour the cream into the pan, stirring well to heat through, and season with salt and pepper. Add the sliced sausage and heat gently for 2 minutes. Pour the sauce over the pasta and serve.

Preparation time: 10 minutes
Cooking time: 10 minutes

SAUSAGE AND PEPPER RISOTTO

This is made with traditional risotto rice – it gives a very creamy result, so don't worry if the finished dish seems a bit sticky!

Serves 2

Ingredients	Metric	Imperial	American
Vegetable oil	15 ml	1 tbsp	1 tbsp
Sausages, cut into chunks	4	4	4
Onion, sliced	1	1	1
Red (bell) pepper, sliced	1	1	1
Green pepper, sliced	1	1	1
Risotto rice	150 g	5 oz	⅔ cup
Can of tomatoes, chopped	400 g	14 oz	1 large
Chicken or vegetable stock	200 ml	7 fl oz	scant 1 cup
Courgette (zucchini), sliced	1	1	1
Paprika	5 ml	1 tsp	1 tsp
Salt and freshly ground black pepper			

1 Heat the oil in a large frying pan (skillet) and fry (sauté) the sausages and onion for 3 minutes until the sausages are lightly browned.

2 Add all the remaining ingredients and season well. Bring the mixture to the boil, cover and simmer for 15–20 minutes or until all the liquid has been absorbed.

Preparation time: 5 minutes
Cooking time: 20 minutes

TAGLIATELLE WITH SAUSAGE AND PESTO

Pesto is a traditional Italian sauce made from basil, garlic, pine nuts, olive oil and Parmesan and the good news is that it comes ready-made in jars! Red pesto gets its colour and rich flavour from sun-dried tomatoes.

Serves 2

Ingredients	Metric	Imperial	American
Tagliatelle	200 g	7 oz	7 oz
Smoked pork sausage, sliced	100 g	4 oz	4 oz
Green or red pesto	60 ml	4 tbsp	4 tbsp
Single (light) cream	150 ml	¼ pt	⅔ cup
Salt and freshly ground black pepper			
Grated cheese and extra black pepper, to serve			

1   Cook the pasta in boiling water according to the packet instructions. Drain and return to the pan.

2   Stir in the remaining ingredients, seasoning to taste.

3   Serve with grated cheese and lots of black pepper.

Preparation time: 10 minutes
Cooking time: 5 minutes

EGGY MACARONI CHEESE

Serves 2

Ingredients	Metric	Imperial	American
Macaroni	175 g	6 oz	6 oz
Cheese sauce (see page 19)	600 ml	1 pt	2½ cups
Eggs, hard-boiled (hard-cooked)	2	2	2
Cheddar cheese, grated	60 ml	4 tbsp	4 tbsp
Tomatoes, sliced	2	2	2

1 Cook the macaroni in boiling water according to the packet instructions. Drain and spoon into an ovenproof dish.

2 Pour the cheese sauce over the macaroni. Chop the eggs into small pieces and stir into the macaroni.

3 Top with the cheese and tomatoes and bake in a preheated oven at 180°C/350°F/gas mark 4 for 20 minutes until golden brown.

Preparation time: 10 minutes
Cooking time: 20 minutes

SAUSAGE AND MUSHROOM PASTA BAKE

Serves 2

Ingredients	Metric	Imperial	American
Pasta shapes	175 g	6 oz	6 oz
Butter or margarine	25 g	1 oz	2 tbsp
Mushrooms, sliced	225 g	8 oz	8 oz
Cooked sausages, sliced	4	4	4
Pesto	45 ml	3 tbsp	3 tbsp
Tomato purée (paste)	30 ml	2 tbsp	2 tbsp
Salt and freshly ground black pepper			
Cheddar cheese, grated	45 ml	3 tbsp	3 tbsp

1   Cook the pasta shapes in boiling water according to the packet instructions. Drain and place in an ovenproof serving dish.

2   Meanwhile, heat the butter or margarine in a small pan and cook the mushrooms for 3–5 minutes until soft.

3   Add the mushrooms and their cooking liquid to the pasta and stir well. Stir in the sausage slices, pesto and tomato purée, season with salt and pepper and stir well.

4   Top with the grated cheese and bake in a preheated oven at 180°C/350°F/gas mark 4 for 15 minutes or until the cheese turns golden brown.

Preparation time: 10 minutes
Cooking time: 15 minutes

CHEAT'S PAELLA

Paella is a traditional Spanish dish made with rice cooked with chicken portions, prawns and sausages, but this version uses cooked meat and sausages and a touch of turmeric to give that distinctive yellow colour (you should use saffron, but it's very expensive).

Serves 2

Ingredients	Metric	Imperial	American
Vegetable oil	15 ml	1 tbsp	1 tbsp
Onion, chopped	1	1	1
Garlic clove, crushed	1	1	1
White rice	2 mugs	2 mugs	2 mugs
Ground turmeric	2.5 ml	½ tsp	½ tsp
Chicken stock	4 mugs	4 mugs	4 mugs
Salt and freshly ground black pepper			
Red (bell) pepper, sliced	½	½	½
Frozen peas	45 ml	3 tbsp	3 tbsp
Cooked chicken, chopped	100 g	4 oz	1 cup
Chorizo sausage, sliced	75 g	3 oz	3 oz

1   Heat the oil in a large saucepan and fry (sauté) the onion and garlic for 3–5 minutes until soft.

2   Add the rice and turmeric and cook for 1 minute, stirring continuously.

3   Add the stock to the pan, stir well, season with salt and pepper and bring to the boil. Cover and simmer for 5 minutes. Add the pepper and peas and cook for another 5 minutes.

4 Stir in the chicken and sausage and cook for another 5 minutes, stirring occasionally.

 Preparation time: 15 minutes
Cooking time: 15 minutes

TIP: If you've got any leftover cooked meat (bacon or ham works well) or fish (canned tuna and salmon are good), just add it in 5 minutes before the end of the cooking time to heat it right through.

MORE MAIN MEALS

FEED ME

There are enough main courses here to have a different meal every day for three weeks! So get your pen and paper out to write your shopping list and decide which recipe you're going to start with tonight ...

SAUSAGE FAJITAS

**Use any type of meat or vegetarian sausages –
they all work well in this recipe.**

Serves 2

Ingredients	Metric	Imperial	American
Vegetable oil	15 ml	1 tbsp	1 tbsp
Onion, chopped	1	1	1
Garlic cloves, crushed	2	2	2
Sausages, sliced into chunks	4	4	4
Chilli powder	10 ml	2 tsp	2 tsp
Green (bell) pepper, chopped	1	1	1
Red pepper, chopped	1	1	1
Flour tortillas	4	4	4
Plain yoghurt	60 ml	4 tbsp	4 tbsp
Spicy salsa	60 ml	4 tbsp	4 tbsp
Cheddar cheese, grated	75 g	3 oz	3 oz

1 Heat the oil in a medium frying pan (skillet), add the onion and garlic and fry (sauté) over a medium heat for 3–5 minutes until soft.

2 Add the sausage chunks and chilli powder and fry for 5 minutes. Add the peppers and cook for 5 minutes.

3 Meanwhile, heat the tortillas according to the packet instructions.

4 Spread each tortilla with yoghurt and salsa, top with the sausage mixture and grated cheese and roll up to serve.

**Preparation time: 10 minutes
Cooking time: 15 minutes**

BEER-BRAISED SAUSAGES WITH CHILLI POTATOES

Brown ale gives a wonderful flavour to this dish – and you don't need to use the whole bottle, so you can drink the rest while you're cooking!

Serves 2

Ingredients	Metric	Imperial	American
New potatoes, scrubbed	700 g	1½ lb	1½ lb
Vegetable oil	45 ml	3 tbsp	3 tbsp
Pork and herb sausages	4	4	4
Onion, chopped	1	1	1
Tomato purée (paste)	15 ml	1 tbsp	1 tbsp
Plain (all-purpose) flour	30 ml	2 tbsp	2 tbsp
Brown ale	300 ml	½ pt	1¼ cups
Water	150 ml	¼ pt	⅔ cup
Dried mixed herbs	15 ml	1 tbsp	1 tbsp
Sugar	10 ml	2 tsp	2 tsp
Salt and freshly ground black pepper			
Red chilli, seeded and chopped	1	1	1
Butter	25 g	1 oz	2 tbsp

1 Boil the potatoes in salted water for 15 minutes until soft.

2 Meanwhile, heat 15 ml/1 tbsp of the oil in a frying pan (skillet) and fry (sauté) the sausages for 5–10 minutes until browned, then remove from the pan.

3 Add the remaining oil and fry the onion for 3 minutes until soft. Add the tomato purée and cook for 1 minute. Stir in the flour and cook for 1 minute. Gradually add half the ale and the water, stirring all the time.

4   Add the herbs, sugar and the remaining ale and season with salt and pepper. Return the sausages to the pan and cook for 10–12 minutes.

5   Meanwhile, drain the cooked potatoes and lightly mash them with a fork, season with salt and pepper and stir in the chilli and butter. Serve the chilli mash with the sausages and sauce.

 Preparation time: 15 minutes
Cooking time: 10–12 minutes

SPEEDY SAUSAGE PIZZA

The quantities here will top a 25 cm/10 in pizza base. For variety, try adding sliced (bell) peppers, tuna, olives, mushrooms, sweetcorn (corn), spinach, ham, fresh herbs or whatever you fancy!

Serves 1

Ingredients	Metric	Imperial	American
Ready-made tomato sauce	90 ml	6 tbsp	6 tbsp
Ready-made pizza base	1	1	1
Cooked sausages, sliced	3	3	3
Mozzarella cheese, sliced	50 g	2 oz	½ cup

Spread the sauce over the pizza base, top with the sausages and cheese and bake according to the instructions on the pizza base packet.

 Preparation time: 5 minutes
Cooking time: 10–15 minutes

TOAD IN THE HOLE

You can use all milk for the batter if you prefer.

Serves 4

Ingredients	Metric	Imperial	American
Sausages	8	8	8
Plain (all-purpose) flour	100 g	4 oz	1 cup
Salt	5 ml	1 tsp	1 tsp
Eggs, beaten	2	2	2
Milk	150 ml	¼ pt	⅔ cup
Water	150 ml	¼ pt	⅔ cup

1 Preheat the oven to 220°C/425°F/gas mark 7. Cut the
sausages in half, place in a medium-sized roasting tin
(pan) and cook in the oven for 10 minutes.

2 To make the batter, place the flour and salt in a mixing
bowl, and stir the eggs into the flour. Gradually add
the milk, whisking all the time, then slowly add the
water to form a smooth, runny batter.

3 Remove the tin from the oven and pour the batter
over the sausages. Return to the oven and cook for
20 minutes or until the Yorkshire pudding is well risen
and golden brown.

 Preparation time: 10 minutes
Cooking time: 20 minutes

TIP: For extra flavour, fry (sauté) some sliced onions in a
little oil until lightly golden brown and spoon them
over the top when you serve the Toad in the Hole.

SAUSAGE CHILLI

Serves 2

Ingredients	Metric	Imperial	American
Vegetable oil	15 ml	1 tbsp	1 tbsp
Sausages	4	4	4
Onion, chopped	1	1	1
Garlic clove, crushed	1	1	1
Can of tomatoes, chopped	400 g	14 oz	1 large
Can of baked beans in tomato sauce	400 g	14 oz	1 large
Chilli powder	10 ml	2 tsp	2 tsp
Tomato purée (paste)	15 ml	1 tbsp	1 tbsp
Boiled rice or jacket potatoes, to serve			

1 Heat the oil in a frying pan (skillet) and fry (sauté) the sausages, onion and garlic for 5 minutes until the sausages are lightly browned and the onion is soft. Chop the sausage into chunks.

2 Add all the remaining ingredients to the pan and cook for 10–15 minutes. Serve with boiled rice or a jacket potato.

Preparation time: 5 minutes
Cooking time: 10–15 minutes

VEGETABLE KORMA

Try this with naan bread flavoured with coriander (cilantro) and garlic (available in most supermarkets).

Serves 2

Ingredients	Metric	Imperial	American
Small cauliflower florets	6	6	6
Carrot, sliced	1	1	1
Potatoes, cut into chunks	2	2	2
Vegetable oil	30 ml	2 tbsp	2 tbsp
Onion, chopped	1	1	1
Garlic clove, crushed	1	1	1
Mild curry powder	30 ml	2 tbsp	2 tbsp
Can of butter (lima) beans, drained	400 g	14 oz	1 large
Can of tomatoes, drained and juice reserved	400 g	14 oz	1 large
Creamed coconut, chopped into small pieces	50 g	2 oz	2 oz
Carton of plain yoghurt	150 g	5 oz	1 small
Salt and freshly ground black pepper			
Boiled rice or naan bread, to serve			

1 Cook the cauliflower, carrots and potatoes in boiling salted water until just tender.

2 Heat the oil in a large frying pan (skillet) and fry (sauté) the onion and garlic for 3–5 minutes until soft.

3 Stir in the curry powder and cook for 1 minute.

4   Add the cooked vegetables, butter beans and reserved tomato juice. (Keep the tomatoes for use in another dish). Add the creamed coconut and stir until dissolved.

5   Stir in the yoghurt, heat through and season to taste with salt and pepper before serving with boiled rice or naan bread.

Preparation time: **20** minutes
Cooking time: **10** minutes

BEAN BURRITOS

Flour tortillas filled with a tasty mix of vegetables and beans and topped with melted cheese – a vegetarian feast!

Serves 2

Ingredients	Metric	Imperial	American
Flour tortillas	4	4	4
Vegetable oil	15 ml	1 tbsp	1 tbsp
Onion, chopped	1	1	1
Garlic clove, crushed	1	1	1
Can of tomatoes, chopped	200 g	7 oz	1 small
Can of red kidney beans, drained	200 g	7 oz	1 small
Spinach, chopped	100 g	4 oz	4 oz
Sugar	5 ml	1 tsp	1 tsp
Tomato purée (paste)	15 ml	1 tbsp	1 tbsp
Cheddar cheese, grated	50 g	2 oz	½ cup

1 Heat the tortillas according to the packet instructions and keep them warm.

2 Heat the oil in a frying pan (skillet), add the onion and garlic and fry (sauté) for 3–5 minutes until soft.

3 Add all the remaining ingredients except the cheese and cook gently for 5 minutes or until the spinach is cooked.

4 Divide the mixture between the tortillas, roll up and arrange in a single layer in a flameproof dish. Sprinkle with the cheese. Grill (broil) for a few minutes until the cheese is golden and bubbling.

Preparation time: 15 minutes
Cooking time: 15 minutes

CHINESE-STYLE SAUSAGE KEBABS

Serves 2

Ingredients	Metric	Imperial	American
Cocktail sausages	8	8	8
Red (bell) pepper, cut into chunks ½	½	½	
Green pepper, cut into chunks ½	½	½	
Can of pineapple chunks, drained and juice reserved	200 g	7 oz	1 small
Clear honey	15 ml	1 tbsp	1 tbsp
Soy sauce	15 ml	1 tbsp	1 tbsp
Tomato purée (paste)	15 ml	1 tbsp	1 tbsp
Salt and freshly ground black pepper			

1 Thread the sausages and chunks of pepper and pineapple on to four skewers (see Tip below).

2 Mix together the honey, soy sauce and tomato purée with 30 ml/2 tbsp of the reserved pineapple juice. Season with salt and pepper.

3 Preheat the grill (broiler) and brush each kebab with the glaze. Cook the kebabs for 10 minutes, turning and spooning any extra glaze over the top as they cook.

Preparation time: 10 minutes
Cooking time: 10 minutes

TIP: You can use metal or wooden skewers, but if you use wooden ones soak them in cold water for 15 minutes before you start cooking – this stops them from burning.

BANGERS WITH ONION GRAVY

Serves 2

Ingredients	Metric	Imperial	American
Vegetable oil	30 ml	2 tbsp	2 tbsp
Onions, sliced	4	4	4
Sausages	4	4	4
Plain (all-purpose) flour	15 ml	1 tbsp	1 tbsp
Chicken stock	300 ml	½ pt	1¼ cups
Salt and freshly ground black pepper			
Mashed potato, to serve			

1   Heat the oil in a small frying pan (skillet) and gently fry (sauté) the onions for 15–20 minutes until they turn a dark brown colour, stirring occasionally. Do not turn the heat up too high or the onions will burn.

2   Meanwhile, grill (broil) the sausages under a preheated grill (broiler) for 10–15 minutes or until cooked.

3   When the onions are cooked, stir in the flour, then gradually add the stock until the gravy is as thick as you want it. Season to taste with salt and pepper.

4   Serve the sausages with mashed potato and plenty of Onion Gravy.

Preparation time: 10 minutes
Cooking time: 20 minutes

TIP: For extra-tasty mashed potato, stir in one of the following: 2 crushed garlic cloves, 30 ml/2 tbsp pesto or 15 ml/1 tbsp wholegrain mustard.

HONEY-GRILLED SAUSAGES WITH CHILLI MASH

Serves 2

Ingredients	Metric	Imperial	American
Potatoes, chopped	700 g	1½ lb	1½ lb
Clear honey	30 ml	2 tbsp	2 tbsp
Chilli sauce	45 ml	3 tbsp	3 tbsp
Pork sausages	4	4	4
Butter or margarine	25 g	1 oz	2 tbsp
Milk	45 ml	3 tbsp	3 tbsp

1 Bring a pan of salted water to the boil and cook the potatoes until softened.

2 Mix together the honey and 15 ml/1 tbsp of the chilli sauce.

3 Cook the sausages under a preheated grill (broiler) for about 10 minutes, turning frequently. Spoon the honey and chilli mixture over them and cook for a further 5 minutes until cooked through.

4 Drain and mash the potatoes and stir in the butter or margarine and milk and the remaining chilli sauce. Serve with the sausages.

Preparation time: 15 minutes
Cooking time: 15 minutes

CHEESY LENTIL AND POTATO BAKE

Serves 2

Ingredients	Metric	Imperial	American
Red lentils	50 g	2 oz	⅓ cup
Water	150 ml	¼ pt	⅔ cup
Butter or margarine	25 g	1 oz	2 tbsp
Onion, chopped	1	1	1
Mushrooms, sliced	50 g	2 oz	2 oz
Plain (all-purpose) flour	15 ml	1 tbsp	1 tbsp
Tomato purée (paste)	15 ml	1 tbsp	1 tbsp
Milk	150 ml	¼ pt	⅔ cup
Salt and freshly ground black pepper			
Medium potatoes, cooked and sliced	3	3	3
Cheddar cheese, grated	50 g	2 oz	½ cup

1 Cook the lentils in the water for about 20 minutes until they are tender and all the water has been absorbed.

2 Melt the butter or margarine in a small saucepan and fry (sauté) the onion for 3–5 minutes. Add the mushrooms and cook for 2–3 minutes.

3 Add the flour to the pan and stir well. Stir in the tomato purée and gradually add the milk, stirring continuously.

4   Stir the lentils into the sauce and season to taste with salt and pepper. Pour the sauce into an ovenproof dish and top with the potato slices and the grated cheese.

5   Bake in a preheated oven at 200°C/400°F/gas mark 6 for 15–20 minutes or until golden brown.

Preparation time: 20 minutes
Cooking time: 20 minutes

HOT ROAST POTATO SALAD WITH PESTO DIP

Serves 2

Ingredients	Metric	Imperial	American
Vegetable oil	60 ml	4 tbsp	4 tbsp
New potatoes, scrubbed and cut into chunks	450 g	1 lb	1 lb
Salt and freshly ground black pepper			
Leek, sliced	1	1	1
Red (bell) pepper, sliced	1	1	1
Green pepper, sliced	1	1	1
Garlic cloves, crushed	2	2	2
Red chilli, seeded and chopped	1	1	1
Dried rosemary	5 ml	1 tsp	1 tsp
Smoked pork sausage, sliced	100 g	4 oz	4 oz
Mayonnaise	60 ml	4 tbsp	4 tbsp
Pesto	15 ml	1 tbsp	1 tbsp

1 Preheat the oven to 200°C/400°F/gas mark 6. Pour the oil into a roasting tin (pan) and place in the oven for 5 minutes.

2 Remove the tin from the oven, add the potatoes and stir well to ensure all the potatoes are coated in the oil. Season well with salt and pepper and cook for 15 minutes.

3 Add the leek, peppers, garlic, chilli and rosemary, stir well and return to the oven for 30 minutes. When the vegetables are cooked through, add the sausage to the mixture, stir well and return to the oven for 10 minutes.

4 Mix the mayonnaise and pesto together in a small bowl
and serve as a dip with the Hot Roast Potato Salad.

 »› Preparation time: 10 minutes
Cooking time: 55 minutes

MEXICAN SAUSAGE TACOS

Serves 2

Ingredients	Metric	Imperial	American
Sausages	4	4	4
Taco shells	4	4	4
Taco sauce	60–90 ml	4–6 tbsp	4–6 tbsp
Lettuce leaves, shredded	8–10	8–10	8–10
Red (bell) pepper, sliced	½	½	½
Cheddar cheese, grated	60 ml	4 tbsp	4 tbsp
Greek yoghurt or soured (dairy sour) cream	60 ml	4 tbsp	4 tbsp

1 Cook the sausages under a preheated grill (broiler) for
10–12 minutes.

2 Warm the taco shells and the taco sauce according to
the packet instructions.

3 Place a layer of lettuce and sliced pepper in the bottom
of each shell. Add the cooked sausages and top with
the warmed sauce, grated cheese and yoghurt or
soured cream.

 »› Preparation time: 5 minutes
Cooking time: 10–12 minutes

SPICY BEAN PIE

This is great for using up any leftover mash. The quantity
doesn't matter, so use as much as you want, but make sure
it covers the bean mixture. If you need to make it from
scratch, prepare and cook two large potatoes before you
make the bean filling.

Serves 2

Ingredients	Metric	Imperial	American
Vegetable oil	15 ml	1 tbsp	1 tbsp
Onion, chopped	1	1	1
Can of tomatoes, chopped	400 g	14 oz	1 large
Can of butter (lima) beans, drained	400 g	14 oz	1 large
Can of cannellini beans, drained	400 g	14 oz	1 large
Chilli powder	5 ml	1 tsp	1 tsp
Mashed potato, for topping			
Cheddar cheese, grated	45 ml	3 tbsp	3 tbsp

1 Heat the oil in a flameproof casserole (Dutch oven) and
fry (sauté) the onion for 5 minutes until soft.

2 Add the tomatoes, beans and chilli powder and cook
for 5 minutes.

3 Spoon enough mash over to cover the beans well and
top with the cheese.

4 Bake in a preheated oven at 200°C/400°F/gas mark 6
for 15 minutes until the cheese is golden and the
potato is piping hot.

Preparation time: 15 minutes
Cooking time: 15 minutes

APPLE AND SAUSAGE BURGERS

Serves 2

Ingredients	Metric	Imperial	American
Sausagemeat	250 g	9 oz	9 oz
Onion, chopped	1	1	1
Eating (dessert) apple, peeled and chopped	1	1	1
Dried sage	5 ml	1 tsp	1 tsp
Salt and freshly ground black pepper			
Plain (all-purpose) flour	60 ml	4 tbsp	4 tbsp
Wholemeal rolls, mayonnaise and relishes, to serve			

1 Mix together the sausagemeat, onion, apple and sage and season with salt and pepper. Form into four even-sized rounds. Coat each burger in flour.

2 Heat the oil in a large frying pan (skillet) and fry (sauté) the burgers for 5–7 minutes on each side.

3 Spread the rolls with mayonnaise and relishes and place a burger in each roll.

Preparation time: 5 minutes
Cooking time: 15 minutes

TIP: Sprinkle a little grated cheese on each burger at the end of the cooking time and grill (broil) for 2–3 minutes or until the cheese starts to bubble.

MEATBALLS WITH TOMATO SAUCE

Serves 2

Ingredients	Metric	Imperial	American
Vegetable oil	60 ml	4 tbsp	4 tbsp
Onion, chopped	1	1	1
Sausagemeat	250 g	9 oz	9 oz
Dried sage	5 ml	1 tsp	1 tsp
Salt and freshly ground black pepper			
Passata (sieved tomatoes)	200 g	7 oz	scant 1 cup
Dried basil	5 ml	1 tsp	1 tsp
Green (bell) pepper, chopped	½	½	½
Spaghetti or rice and grated cheese, to serve			

1 Heat 15 ml/1 tbsp of the oil in a large frying pan (skillet) and fry (sauté) the onion for 5 minutes until soft. Remove the onion from the pan.

2 Put the sausagemeat in a mixing bowl and add half the onion and the sage. Season with salt and pepper and mix well. Shape the mixture into four even-sized balls.

3 Heat the remaining oil in the frying pan and fry the meatballs for 5–10 minutes until browned. Add the remaining onion, the passata, basil and pepper to the pan, cover and simmer for 10 minutes.

4 Place the meatballs on a bed of spaghetti or rice, pour over the sauce and top with grated cheese.

Preparation time: 15 minutes
Cooking time: 15–20 minutes

CURRIED SAUSAGE STIR-FRY

Serves 2

Ingredients	Metric	Imperial	American
Pork sausages	4	4	4
Vegetable oil	15 ml	1 tbsp	1 tbsp
New potatoes, cooked	275 g	10 oz	10 oz
Green cabbage, chopped	100 g	4 oz	4 oz
Cherry tomatoes, halved	8	8	8
Can of tomatoes, chopped	200 g	7 oz	1 small
Curry paste	15 ml	1 tbsp	1 tbsp
Lemon juice	15 ml	1 tbsp	1 tbsp
Tomato ketchup (catsup)	30 ml	2 tbsp	2 tbsp

1 Cook the sausages under a preheated grill (broiler) for 10–12 minutes. Cut into chunks.

2 Heat the vegetable oil in a frying pan (skillet) and stir-fry the sausages, potatoes and cabbage for 1–2 minutes.

3 Add the remaining ingredients and cook, stirring, for 3–5 minutes until the cabbage is heated right through and lightly cooked but still crisp.

Preparation time: 5 minutes
Cooking time: 20 minutes

CRUNCHY BEAN AND SAUSAGE PIE

An easy pie, topped with tortilla chips for an authentic Mexican touch.

Serves 2

Ingredients	Metric	Imperial	American
Sausages	4	4	4
Vegetable oil	15 ml	1 tbsp	1 tbsp
Onion, sliced	1	1	1
Red (bell) pepper, sliced	½	½	½
Green pepper, sliced	½	½	½
White wine vinegar	15 ml	1 tbsp	1 tbsp
Tomato ketchup (catsup)	30 ml	2 tbsp	2 tbsp
Chilli powder	5 ml	1 tsp	1 tsp
Dried oregano	5 ml	1 tsp	1 tsp
Can of beans in spicy sauce or baked beans in tomato sauce	400 g	14 oz	1 large
Tortilla chips, for topping			
Cheddar cheese, grated	25 g	1 oz	¼ cup

1 Cook the sausages under a preheated grill (broiler) for 10–12 minutes, then cut into slices.

2 Heat the oil in a flameproof casserole (Dutch oven) and stir-fry the sausage slices, onion and peppers for 5 minutes.

3 Add the vinegar, ketchup, chilli and oregano and cook for 1–2 minutes. Stir in the beans.

4 Cover the bean and sausage mixture with tortilla chips and sprinkle with the grated cheese. Bake in a preheated oven at 180°C/350°F/gas mark 4 for 20 minutes.

**Preparation time: 20 minutes
Cooking time: 20 minutes**

SAUSAGE AND RED CABBAGE STIR-FRY

Serves 2

Ingredients	Metric	Imperial	American
Cumberland or vegetarian sausages	4	4	4
Red cabbage, sliced	225 g	8 oz	8 oz
Vegetable oil	15 ml	1 tbsp	1 tbsp
Onion, chopped	1	1	1
Eating (dessert) apple, sliced but not peeled	1	1	1
Sultanas (golden raisins)	50 g	2 oz	⅓ cup
Apple juice	150 ml	¼ pt	⅔ cup
Vinegar	10 ml	2 tsp	2 tsp
Sugar	10 ml	2 tsp	2 tsp

1 Cook the sausages under a preheated grill (broiler) for 10–12 minutes. Cut into chunks.

2 Cook the cabbage in boiling water for 2 minutes, then drain well.

3 Heat the oil in a large frying pan (skillet) and stir-fry the sausages and onion for 2 minutes until the sausages are lightly browned.

4 Add the cabbage and apple and stir-fry for 2 minutes. Add all the remaining ingredients and stir-fry for 3–4 minutes.

Preparation time: 5 minutes
Cooking time: 20 minutes

CRISPY SAGE AND SAUSAGE BAKE

Serves 2–3

Ingredients	Metric	Imperial	American
Onion, chopped	1	1	1
Carrot, sliced	1	1	1
Eating (dessert) apple, chopped	1	1	1
Plain (all-purpose) flour	15 ml	1 tbsp	1 tbsp
Paprika	5 ml	1 tsp	1 tsp
Salt and freshly ground black pepper			
Sausagemeat	450 g	1 lb	1 lb
Dried sage	5 ml	1 tsp	1 tsp
Garlic clove, crushed	1	1	1
Pototoes, cooked and sliced	450 g	1 lb	1 lb

1　Mix together the onion, carrot and apple and place in an ovenproof dish. Sprinkle with the flour, paprika and plenty of salt and pepper.

2　Mix together the sausagemeat, sage and garlic and spread over the vegetables.

3　Top with the sliced potatoes and bake in a preheated oven at 190°C/375°F/gas mark 5 for 40 minutes or until the potatoes are golden and crisp.

 Preparation time: 10 minutes
Cooking time: 40 minutes

BAKED SPANISH EGGS

Serves 2

Ingredients	Metric	Imperial	American
Vegetable oil	15 ml	1 tbsp	1 tbsp
Slices of ham, chopped	3	3	3
Onion, chopped	1	1	1
Can of tomatoes, drained and chopped	400 g	14 oz	1 large
Frozen peas, cooked	50 g	2 oz	2 oz
Potatoes, cooked and sliced	225 g	8 oz	8 oz
Green (bell) pepper, sliced	1	1	1
Chorizo, sliced	175 g	6 oz	6 oz
Eggs	4	4	4

1 Heat the oil in a frying pan (skillet) and fry (sauté) the ham and onion for 5 minutes. Stir in the tomatoes, peas, potatoes and pepper and cook for 5 minutes. Stir in the chorizo.

2 Pour the sausage and vegetable mixture into a shallow ovenproof dish. Make four indents into the mixture with a tablespoon and break an egg into each one.

3 Bake in a preheated oven at 230°C/450°F/gas mark 8 for 2–3 minutes or until the eggs are cooked.

Preparation time: 10 minutes
Cooking time: 3 minutes

Whoever you're trying to impress – new girlfriend, boyfriend, flatmates or even your parents – here is a selection of main courses and desserts that are a bit special but still easy to put together. Some take a little longer than the other recipes in the book, but that's usually because the dish is cooking itself in the oven, which means you can go and have a shower and relax before you serve up your masterpiece.

HADDOCK AND BEAN CHOWDER

This main course soup is a real treat – if you're feeling extravagant, make it with half salmon and half haddock.

Serves 4

Ingredients	Metric	Imperial	American
Vegetable oil	15 ml	1 tbsp	1 tbsp
Leeks, sliced	2	2	2
Carrot, diced	1	1	1
Celery sticks, sliced	2	2	2
Fish stock	900 ml	1½ pt	3¾ cups
Milk	300 ml	½ pt	1¼ cups
Potatoes, diced	2	2	2
Smoked haddock, skinned and cubed	450 g	1 lb	1 lb
Can of butter (lima) beans, drained	400 g	14 oz	1 large
Dried parsley	10 ml	2 tsp	2 tsp
Lemon juice	5 ml	1 tsp	1 tsp
Double (heavy) cream	60 ml	4 tbsp	4 tbsp
Pesto	30 ml	2 tbsp	2 tbsp
Ciabatta or focaccia bread, to serve			

1   Heat the oil in a large pan over a low heat and cook the leek, carrot and celery until softened. Add the stock and milk and bring to a gentle simmer.

2   Add the diced potato and simmer for 5–8 minutes until the potato is just cooked. Add the haddock to the pan and cook for 2–3 minutes. Add the beans, parsley and lemon juice to the pan and cook for 2 minutes. Season to taste. Ladle into bowls, stir in the double cream and top with a dollop of pesto.

3   Serve with ciabatta or focaccia bread.

Preparation time: 10 minutes
Cooking time: 20 minutes

TIP: Soak the sliced leeks in cold water for 10 minutes before cooking to draw out any soil trapped between the layers.

SAUSAGES IN RED WINE

It really is worth sacrificing a bottle of red in this tasty dish when you'd probably rather drink it! You don't need to splash out on the best wine, but do buy the best sausages you can afford.

Serves 4

Ingredients	Metric	Imperial	American
Butter or margarine	25 g	1 oz	2 tbsp
Vegetable oil	30 ml	2 tbsp	2 tbsp
Sausages	8	8	8
Onion, chopped	1	1	1
Plain (all-purpose) flour	15 ml	1 tbsp	1 tbsp
Red wine	400 ml	14 fl oz	1¾ cups
Garlic clove, crushed	1	1	1
Dried thyme	5 ml	1 tsp	1 tsp
Dried sage	5 ml	1 tsp	1 tsp
Salt and freshly ground black pepper			
Mushrooms, sliced	200 g	7 oz	7 oz
Mashed potatoes, to serve			

1 Melt the butter or margarine in a flameproof casserole (Dutch oven), add the oil and fry (sauté) the sausages for a few minutes until browned all over. With a slotted spoon, remove the sausages from the casserole and put on a plate.

2 Add the onion to the casserole and fry until soft, then stir in the flour. Gradually add the wine, stirring all the time.

3 Put the sausages back in the casserole with the garlic, thyme and sage. Season with salt and pepper. Cover and simmer very gently for 30 minutes.

4 Add the mushrooms and cook for another 20 minutes, then serve with mashed potatoes.

Preparation time: 15 minutes
Cooking time: 50 minutes

PORK AND APPLE CASSEROLE

Serves 4

Ingredients	Metric	Imperial	American
Vegetable oil	45 ml	3 tbsp	3 tbsp
Stewing pork, cubed	450 g	1 lb	1 lb
Onion, chopped	1	1	1
Garlic clove, crushed	1	1	1
Ground coriander (cilantro)	15 ml	1 tbsp	1 tbsp
Ground cumin	15 ml	1 tbsp	1 tbsp
Plain (all-purpose) flour	30 ml	2 tbsp	2 tbsp
Apple juice	150 ml	¼ pt	⅔ cup
Cider	300 ml	½ pt	1¼ cups
Salt and freshly ground black pepper			
Can of butter (lima) beans, drained	400 g	14 oz	1 large
Eating (dessert) apples, chopped but not peeled	2	2	2
Single (light) cream	150 ml	¼ pt	⅔ cup
Boiled brown rice and green vegetables, to serve			

1 Heat the oil in an ovenproof casserole (Dutch oven) and fry (sauté) the pork for a few minutes until browned. Remove from the pan.

2 Add the onion and garlic to the casserole and cook for 3 minutes. Add the spices and flour and cook for 2 minutes, stirring continuously.

3 Turn down the heat and add the apple juice and cider. Season well with salt and pepper. Add the pork and beans to the pan and bring to the boil. Cover and cook in a preheated oven at 160°C/325°F/gas mark 3 for 1¼ hours.

4 Stir the apples into the casserole and cook for another 15 minutes. Stir the cream into the casserole and serve with brown rice and green vegetables.

 Preparation time: 20 minutes
Cooking time: 1½ hours

STUFFED PEPPERS

These look really impressive but are actually really easy to make – ideal!

Serves 4

Ingredients	Metric	Imperial	American
(Bell) peppers, any colour	4	4	4
Can of butter (lima) beans, drained	400 g	14 oz	1 large
Pine nuts	50 g	2 oz	½ cup
Red chilli, seeded and finely chopped	1	1	1
Cream cheese with garlic and herbs	225 g	8 oz	1 cup
Salt and freshly ground black pepper			
Passata (sieved tomatoes)	600 ml	1 pt	2½ cups
Fresh basil leaves, to garnish			
Boiled rice and broccoli or mangetout (snow peas), to serve			

1 Using a sharp knife, slice the tops off the peppers and cut out all the white bits and seeds from inside. Trim the bottoms, if necessary, so that they will stand upright, but be careful not to cut right through. Rinse thoroughly and pat dry on kitchen paper (paper towels).

2 Mash the butter beans to form a coarse paste (leave a few beans whole for texture), then stir in the pine nuts, chilli and cream cheese. Season with salt and pepper.

3 Spoon the mixture into the peppers and replace the tops as 'lids'. Pour the passata into an ovenproof casserole (Dutch oven) large enough to hold the peppers standing up.

4 Carefully place the peppers in the dish and cover tightly with foil, moulding the foil to help the peppers stay upright. Bake in a preheated oven at 180°C/350°F/gas mark 4 for 20–30 minutes or until the peppers are cooked through.

5 Garnish with a few fresh basil leaves, then serve with rice and broccoli or mangetout.

Preparation time: **20 minutes**
Cooking time: **30 minutes**

SEAFOOD WRAPS

These are the cheat's version of stuffed pancakes – they use
flour tortillas rather than pancakes. Smoked salmon is
expensive, but you can buy offcuts much more cheaply and
you don't need much to get the delicious flavour.

Serves 4

Ingredients	Metric	Imperial	American
Butter or margarine	25 g	1 oz	2 tbsp
Plain (all-purpose) flour	25 g	1 oz	2 tbsp
Milk	150 ml	¼ pt	⅔ cup
White wine	150 ml	¼ pt	⅔ cup
Cheddar cheese, grated	100 g	4 oz	1 cup
Can of salmon, drained	200 g	7 oz	1 small
Frozen prawns (shrimp), defrosted	100 g	4 oz	4 oz
Egg, hard-boiled (hard-cooked) and chopped	1	1	1
Chopped fresh parsley	30 ml	2 tbsp	2 tbsp
Flour tortillas	8	8	8
Passatta (sieved tomatoes)	300 ml	½ pt	1¼ cups
Crème fraîche	60 ml	4 tbsp	4 tbsp
Smoked salmon, cut into strips	50 g	2 oz	2 oz

1 Melt the butter or margarine in a small saucepan over
a low heat. Stir in the flour and cook for 1 minute,
stirring all the time. Gradually add the milk, stirring
until blended. Stir in the wine, half the cheese, the
canned salmon, prawns, egg and parsley.

2   Divide the mixture between the tortillas, roll up and place in an ovenproof dish. Pour the passata over and sprinkle the remaining cheese on the top.

3   Bake in a preheated oven at 180°C/350°F/gas mark 4 for 10–15 minutes until the sauce is heated right through.

4   Drizzle the crème fraîche over the wraps and arrange the smoked salmon strips over the top, then serve.

Preparation time: 10 minutes
Cooking time: 15 minutes

PAPRIKA BEEF

Serves 4

Ingredients	Metric	Imperial	American
Vegetable oil	30 ml	2 tbsp	2 tbsp
Stewing steak, cubed	450 g	1 lb	1 lb
Onion, chopped	1	1	1
Garlic clove, crushed	1	1	1
Paprika	15 ml	1 tbsp	1 tbsp
Tomato purée (paste)	10 ml	2 tsp	2 tsp
Plain (all-purpose) flour	15 ml	1 tbsp	1 tbsp
Beef stock	450 ml	¾ pt	2 cups
Dried mixed herbs	10 ml	2 tsp	2 tsp
Can of kidney beans, drained	400 g	14 oz	1 large
Salt and freshly ground black pepper			
Green (bell) pepper, sliced	1	1	1
Tomatoes, quartered	2	2	2
Soured (dairy sour) cream	150 ml	¼ pt	⅔ cup
Buttered tagliatelle or noodles, to serve			

1 Heat the oil in a flameproof casserole (Dutch oven) and fry (sauté) the meat on all sides. Remove and drain on kitchen paper (paper towels). Fry the onion and garlic in the oil remaining in the dish.

2 Stir in the paprika, tomato purée and flour. Gradually add the beef stock. Add the herbs and beans and bring to the boil. Return the meat to the dish and season with salt and pepper.

3   Cover and cook in a preheated oven at 150°C/300°F/
    gas mark 2 for 2 hours.

4   Add the pepper and tomatoes and cook for a further
    30 minutes.

5   Stir in the soured cream and serve immediately with
    buttered tagliatelle or noodles.

Preparation time: 15 minutes
Cooking time: 2½ hours

GOATS' CHEESE FILO PARCELS

You can buy packets of frozen filo pastry (paste) in most supermarkets – it's very thin, ready-rolled and really easy to use. Don't forget to leave time to thaw it first!

Serves 4

Ingredients	Metric	Imperial	American
Goats' cheese	200 g	7 oz	7 oz
Sheets of filo pastry, about 30 cm/12 in square	8	8	8
Butter or margarine, melted	75 g	3 oz	⅓ cup
Egg, hard-boiled (hard-cooked) and sliced	1	1	1
Redcurrant jelly (clear conserve)	90 ml	6 tbsp	6 tbsp
Buttered new potatoes and salad or green vegetables, to serve			

1 Divide the goats' cheese into four equal-sized rounds, each about 4 cm/1½ in across.

2 Brush one sheet of pastry with butter or margarine and place another sheet on top. Place a goats' cheese round in the centre of the pastry and top with a slice of egg and 5 ml/1 tsp redcurrant jelly.

3 Pull the corners of the pastry to the centre and squeeze the pastry just above the cheese filling to form a 'moneybag' shape. Repeat with the remaining pastry to make four parcels.

4 Place the parcels on a baking (cookie) sheet and bake in a preheated oven at 180°C/350°F/gas mark 4 for 15–20 minutes or until the pastry is golden brown. Serve the parcels with buttered new potatoes, salad or green vegetables and the remaining redcurrant jelly.

Preparation time: 20 minutes
Cooking time: 15–20 minutes

ITALIAN CHICKEN BAKE

These chicken breasts are particularly good served with Rosemary Potatoes (see page 16). Prepare the potatoes and put them in the oven before you start the chicken recipe.

Serves 4

Ingredients	Metric	Imperial	American
Vegetable oil	15 ml	1 tbsp	1 tbsp
Onion, chopped	1	1	1
Garlic cloves, crushed	2	2	2
Can of tomatoes, chopped	400 g	14 oz	1 large
Red wine	150 ml	¼ pt	⅔ cup
Can of cannellini beans, drained	400 g	14 oz	1 large
Dried basil	10 ml	2 tsp	2 tsp
Chicken breasts	4	4	4
Salt and freshly ground black pepper			
Mozzarella cheese, sliced	100 g	4 oz	1 cup

1 Heat the oil in a flameproof casserole (Dutch oven) and fry (sauté) the onion and garlic for 5 minutes until soft.

2 Add the tomatoes, red wine, cannellini beans and basil, bring to the boil, then simmer for 10 minutes.

3 Add the chicken breasts to the casserole, season with salt and pepper and cover with slices of Mozzarella.

4 Bake in a preheated oven at 200°C/400°F/gas mark 6 for 30 minutes until the chicken is cooked.

Preparation time: 10 minutes
Cooking time: 30 minutes

APRICOT AND AMARETTI TRIFLE

Amaretti biscuits (cookies) are traditional Italian almond biscuits; most supermarkets stock them.

Serves 4

Ingredients	Metric	Imperial	American
Amaretti biscuits	100 g	4 oz	4 oz
Can of apricots, drained and juice reserved	400 g	14 oz	1 large
Sherry	60 ml	4 tbsp	4 tbsp
Can or carton of ready-made custard	400 g	14 oz	1 large
Double (heavy) cream	300 ml	½ pt	1¼ cups

1 Break the amaretti biscuits into small pieces, and place in the base of a serving dish, reserving 30 ml/2 tbsp for decoration.

2 Chop the apricots into chunks and place on top of the biscuits. Mix 60 ml/4 tbsp of the reserved apricot juice with the sherry, then spoon over the fruit.

3 Pour the custard over the fruit and biscuit mixture.

4 Whip the cream until thick and pour over the custard. Sprinkle the remaining biscuit pieces over the cream and chill the trifle in the fridge for at least 1 hour before serving.

Preparation time: 15 minutes plus chilling
Cooking time: None

MERINGUE STRAWBERRY CRUSH

If you can't buy strawberries, this also works well with slices of banana, kiwi fruit or orange.

Serves 4

Ingredients	Metric	Imperial	American
Strawberries	450 g	1 lb	1 lb
Meringues	100 g	4 oz	4 oz
Double (heavy) cream	300 ml	½ pt	1¼ cups

1 Slice the strawberries and place in individual serving dishes or a large serving dish.

2 Break the meringues into small pieces and stir into the strawberries.

3 Whip the cream until thick and stir into the meringue mixture. Chill before serving.

 Preparation time: 15 minutes
Cooking time: None

TIP: For a boozy flavour, add a couple of tablespoons of your favourite spirit – whisky, brandy and any fruit liqueur all work well.

BAKED BANANAS

Milk or white chocolate work just as well in this simple but delicious dish.

Serves 4

Ingredients	Metric	Imperial	American
Bananas	4	4	4
Plain (semi-sweet) chocolate	100 g	4 oz	4 oz
Butter or margarine	25 g	1 oz	2 tbsp
Ground ginger	5 ml	1 tsp	1 tsp
Desiccated (shredded) coconut	60 ml	4 tbsp	4 tbsp
Whipped cream, to serve			

1 Place the bananas in a shallow ovenproof dish. Break the chocolate into small pieces and place on top of the bananas. Chop the butter or margarine into small pieces and add to the dish. Sprinkle the ginger and coconut over the bananas and chocolate.

2 Cover the dish with foil and bake in a preheated oven at 180°C/350°F/gas mark 4 for 20–30 minutes or until the bananas are soft and the chocolate has melted. Serve hot with lots of whipped cream.

Preparation time: 10 minutes
Cooking time: 20–30 minutes

TIP: Try these variations for a change: replace the ginger with 5 ml/1 tsp ground cinnamon; top the pudding with chopped mixed nuts; or sprinkle with finely chopped dried apricots instead of the coconut.

SPEEDY COFFEE CREAMS

These easy creams are made with Mascarpone cheese, a creamy soft Italian cheese which you'll find in tubs in the chiller cabinet at the supermarket.

Serves 4

Ingredients	Metric	Imperial	American
Brown sugar	45 ml	3 tbsp	3 tbsp
Instant coffee granules	25 ml	1½ tbsp	1½ tbsp
Mascarpone cheese	250 g	9 oz	9 oz
Double (heavy) cream	150 ml	¼ pt	⅔ cup
Egg whites (see Tip opposite)	2	2	2
Cocoa (unsweetened chocolate) powder	15–30 ml	1–2 tbsp	1–2 tbsp

1   Place the sugar and coffee granules in a plastic food bag, seal and crush with the back of a spoon.

2   Beat the Mascarpone cheese in a mixing bowl until it is softened, then mix in the coffee and sugar mixture.

3   Whip the cream until thick, then stir it into the Mascarpone cheese.

4   Whisk the egg whites until they stand up in peaks when you pull the whisk away. Mix 30 ml/2 tbsp into the Mascarpone mixture, then carefully stir in the remaining egg white. Spoon the mixture into a serving dish or individual dishes (it looks good in wine glasses) and sprinkle with the cocoa powder.

Preparation time: 10 minutes
Cooking time: None

TIP: To obtain the egg whites you need to separate the eggs.
Break each egg over a small bowl by cracking the shell
with a knife, pull away half of the shell, leaving the yolk
in the other half, and let the white drip into the bowl.
Pass the yolk from one half of the shell to the other,
until all the white has dripped out. It is important not
to let any yolk get into the separated white or you
won't be able to whisk the white.

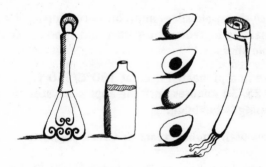

NUTTY APPLE PUDDING

Serves 4

Ingredients	Metric	Imperial	American
Eating (dessert) apples, cored and thinly sliced	3	3	3
Cinnamon	5 ml	1 tsp	1 tsp
Butter or margarine, melted	30 ml	2 tbsp	2 tbsp
Clear honey	15 ml	1 tbsp	1 tbsp
Wholemeal flour	15 ml	1 tbsp	1 tbsp
Chopped mixed nuts	30 ml	2 tbsp	2 tbsp
Soft brown sugar	15 ml	1 tbsp	1 tbsp
Greek yoghurt	30 ml	2 tbsp	2 tbsp
Double (heavy) cream or Greek yoghurt, to serve			

1 Place the apple slices in an ovenproof dish. Mix all the remaining ingredients together and spoon over the apple slices.

2 Bake in a preheated oven at 180°C/350°F/gas mark 4 for 25–30 minutes until the apples are soft and the topping is bubbling.

3 Serve with double cream or Greek yoghurt.

Preparation time: 5 minutes
Cooking time: 25–30 minutes

CHOCOLATE MOUSSE

Serves 4

Ingredients	Metric	Imperial	American
Plain (semi-sweet) chocolate, broken into pieces	225 g	8 oz	2 cups
Eggs, separated (see Tip page 151)	4	4	4
Chopped mixed nuts	30 ml	2 tbsp	2 tbsp
Shortbread biscuits (cookies), to serve			

1   Place a heatproof bowl over a pan of simmering water. Place the chocolate in the bowl and stir until the chocolate melts (don't let any water spill into the chocolate or you'll have to start again).

2   When the chocolate has melted, beat in the egg yolks until thoroughly combined. Leave the mixture to cool for about 15 minutes.

3   Whisk the egg whites until they just hold their shape when you pull the whisk away. Carefully stir the egg whites into the chocolate mixture. Spoon into individual dishes or a large serving dish and sprinkle with chopped nuts.

4   Chill in the fridge for a couple of hours before serving with shortbread biscuits.

Preparation time: 20 minutes plus chilling
Cooking time: 5 minutes

GINGER CREAM ROLL

This is just a packet of ginger biscuits sandwiched together with cream – it looks great, tastes fabulous and is so easy!

Serves 4

Ingredients	Metric	Imperial	American
Ginger biscuits (cookies)	200 g	7 oz	7 oz
Double (heavy) cream, whipped	300 ml	½ pt	1¼ cups
Plain (semi-sweet) chocolate, grated	25 g	1 oz	¼ cup

1 Spread one biscuit with cream, press another biscuit on to it, and place it, standing upright, on a plate. Spread another biscuit and press it on to the second, then continue until you have sandwiched all the biscuits together into a long roll.

2 Cover the whole roll with the remaining cream and sprinkle with the chocolate.

3 Chill in the fridge for at least 1 hour.

4 To serve, cut the roll diagonally into slices.

 Preparation time: 15 minutes plus 1 hour chilling
Cooking time: None

TIP: You can serve this on individual plates if you prefer – just place a few sandwiched biscuits flat on a plate and cover with cream and grated chocolate.

CHEAT'S FRUIT BRULEE

You can make this with drained, canned fruit, such as peaches or apricots instead of the bananas. You will need 400 g/14 oz/1 large can for this recipe.

Serves 4

Ingredients	Metric	Imperial	American
Bananas, sliced	4	4	4
Greek yoghurt	300 ml	½ pt	1¼ cups
Double (heavy) cream, whipped	150 ml	¼ pt	⅔ cup
Soft brown sugar	60 ml	4 tbsp	4 tbsp

1 Divide the sliced bananas between four individual flameproof dishes.

2 Mix together the yoghurt and cream and spoon over the fruit.

3 Preheat the grill (broiler) to high. Sprinkle 15 ml/ 1 tbsp sugar over each dish. Place the dishes under the grill for 3–5 minutes or until the topping melts and turns golden brown, like caramel.

Preparation time: 10 minutes
Cooking time: 5 minutes

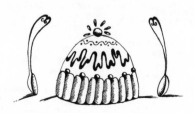

INDEX